www.gabberz.com

Public Speaking for Kids, Tweens, and Teens– Confidence for Life!™

Do-it-Yourself at Home Training Program

"The fun and exciting way for anyone 8 to 18 to develop winning self-confidence and powerful speaking, social engagement, and leadership skills."

Single Student Do-it-Yourself Home Edition

LEVEL 1

First Edition

By David Nemzoff

IMPORTANT NOTE

THIS **SINGLE STUDENT** DO-IT-YOURSELF HOME EDITION IS A SELF-TAUGHT OR **PARENT-ASSISTED** PROGRAM DESIGNED TO HELP YOUTH DEVELOP POWERFUL COMMUNICATION SKILLS. HOWEVER, DUE TO FACTORS SUCH AS DESIRE AND EFFORT, GABBERZ CANNOT PROMISE ANY SPECIFIC OUTCOME OR RESULT. NOTE THAT GABBERZ CAN BE USED BY **ANYONE** OF ANY AGE, HOWEVER <u>YOUNGER CHILDREN WILL NEED SIGNIFICANT PARENTAL ASSISTANCE DOING THE LESSONS</u>. ADULTS, YOU CAN USE THE PROGRAM TOO—IF YOU CAN GET IN FRONT OF AN AUDIENCE OF <u>ONE</u> OR MORE PEOPLE, YOU CAN BECOME A **SUPERHERO SPEAKER!**

Public Speaking for Kids, Tweens, and Teens – Confidence for Life!™: **Level 1, Single Student Intensive Home, First Edition**

ISBN 978-0-9882738-1-8

www.Gabberz.com
www.facebook.com/gabberzone
www.twitter.com/gabberzone
www.youtube.com/gabberztube

673 Potomac Station Drive #710
Leesburg, VA 20176

Table of Contents

Please Read Me!

Welcome to Gabberz public speaking training. Please take a few moments to read the following notes.

STUDENT

1. Don't skip the reading up front (Chapters 1 through 4). It's fun stuff and **will** be helpful.

2. The good news is that **you <u>DO</u> <u>NOT</u> have to memorize (or even understand) all that information.**

3. You'll learn everything step-by-step so there's **no need to memorize** anything in Gabberz. It will all come to your naturally over time.

4. **Seek help** whenever you need it. Your family and friends will be happy to support you.

5. **Get an audience**! Immediate family, extended family, friends, etc. You only need one, but the more people you can get to share your speech events, the more fun and exciting it will be.

6. There is <u>**NO WRONG WAY**</u> for you to do any of the lessons. **So let your inner Ham come out**!

PARENT/INSTRUCTOR

1. **The younger the student, the more you will need to help them.** Students 8 to 10 years old in particular will need your help and support.

2. **You <u>DO NOT</u> have to know anything about public speaking. Every lesson contains all the information needed.**

LOOK!

3. The good news is that **you and the student <u>DO NOT</u> have to memorize (or even understand) all the information we provide.** Everything will be reinforced in lessons so **we don't ask anyone to memorize anything in Gabberz.**

4. The other good news is that there's <u>**NO WRONG WAY**</u> for the student to do any of these lessons. As long as they do the lesson, they are advancing.

5. Help the student get an audience for the speech events. Larger audiences will help the student get more out of the lessons.

6. Most important... **have fun** with the student! It's a great adventure for the entire family.

Now, it's time to get started. Enjoy the adventure and be sure to tell everyone about how much fun Gabberz is. We would love to hear from you.

www.gabberz.com

www.twitter.com/gabberzone

www.facebook.com/gabberzone

www.youtube.com/gabberztube

www.gabberz.com

Public Speaking for Kids, Tweens, and Teens
Level 1, Single-Student, Do-it-Yourself

CHAPTER 1

INTRODUCTION

What You'll Learn in This Chapter:

✓ How does this work?

✓ Why learn to speak in public?

✓ Won't this be embarrassing?

✓ What if I mess up?

PLEASE READ ME !

WE THINK YOU'LL FIND <u>ALL</u> OF THIS INFORMATION INCREDIBLY INTERESTING AND ENTERTAINING. HOWEVER, YOU SHOULD KNOW THAT WE'VE LOADED A LOT OF READING ABOUT PUBLIC SPEAKING UP FRONT IN THE FIRST FOUR CHAPTERS.

AFTER THAT, <u>WE START GETTING TO THE POINT MUCH QUICKER</u> WITH A LOT LESS BACKGROUND MATERIAL AND MORE FUN ACTIVITIES.

SO, HAVE HEART, IF YOU FIND ANY OF THIS BORING (*WE PROMISE WE WON'T CRY IF YOU DO*), KNOW THAT AS YOU MOVE ALONG, WE'LL CONCENTRATE MORE AND MORE ON ACTIONS AND ACTIVITIES THAN ON READING.

AND GUESS WHAT? YOU <u>DON'T HAVE TO MEMORIZE</u> OR EVEN UNDERSTAND ALL THIS STUFF. WE'LL REINFORCE IT THROUGHOUT THE PROGRAM SO YOU DON'T HAVE TO REMEMBER IT NOW. JUST READ IT FOR THE JOY OF READING IT.

WHEN THE TIME COMES THAT YOU NEED ANY OF THIS, WE'LL REMIND YOU ALL ABOUT IT.

HAVE FUN FELLOW GABBERZ!

SERIOUSLY?

I don't have to memorize this stuff?

THAT'S RIGHT!

REALLY?

Sigh...
REALLY!

1   INTRODUCTION

Welcome to Gabberz, the fun way to learn public speaking!

There's nothing to fear here. The program is filled from the bottom to the top with fun, exciting, and unexpected surprises designed to make it easy to be comfortable just being you. You will have to stretch a little as you progress and do new things, but that's what makes it so much fun.

Easy step-by-step methods help you gain confidence in **your** voice and **your** capabilities. Once you get into the program, you'll be seeking out opportunities to stand up and make yourself heard. ***It's not the timid people who make a difference in the world—it's bold people like you.***

And when better to start that adventure than right now!

The exciting thing is that this is **not** just about speaking in public. These skills will help you develop:

- **self-confidence;**

- **the self-assurance to lead;**

- **engaging social interaction skills;**

- **an outgoing personality;**

- **a command leadership presence, and more.**

You may even find the *Inner Ham* in yourselves.

1.1   SO, WHAT IS GABBERZ? HOW DOES IT WORK?

Gabberz is an easy-to-follow, step-by-step program that helps you become comfortable being yourself in front of other people. Whether in front of one person, a small gathering of friends, a family get-together, or a large group, **you decide** how fast you want to work through the program to develop the confidence you want.

You can choose any audience, but you'll generally start with your immediate family. You are encouraged to gather more people for your speeches: family, friends, neighbors, etc. The more people you can gather, the more fun each lesson will be.

Don't worry if your audience is very small in the beginning. **If it makes you more comfortable to speak to an audience of one, that's fine.** As you gain more practice and experience, we believe you will seek out larger audiences.

The process will be simple. When it's time to begin, **you'll start out with a very easy introductory speech we've prepared for you**. You'll see how easy and fun it is and you'll want to jump right into Lesson 1. From there, it only gets more entertaining—with unexpected surprises for both you and your audience.

1.2 "WHY SHOULD I LEARN TO SPEAK IN PUBLIC?"

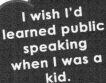

I wish I'd learned public speaking when I was a kid.

"I don't plan on being a politician or an actor. What difference does it make?"

Gabberz is about <u>so much more</u> than just public speaking. It's about feeling confidence in yourself and your ability to express your thoughts. What you have to say has value.

- You've probably been in situations where you wished afterwards that you'd spoken up.

- Or maybe you get frustrated that sometimes **it seems people aren't listening to you**.

- Maybe you're envious of people who always seem to be the center of attention?

- Do you sometimes feel shy or anxious?

- Have people commented that you're 'a quiet kid'?

Speaking confidently is a great and wonderful skill to have. Many adults have a genuine fear of speaking in front of others. By choosing to learn this skill now, you will **not** be one of those who are held back by anxiety and fear. Your speaking ability will give you a great advantage in school, college, job interviews, careers, and social situations. **Often, the winner is *not* who knows the most, it's who *expresses it best*.**

1.3 "SO WHAT... I DON'T PLAN TO SPEAK IN PUBLIC."

No matter what path you take in life, you will need to speak in front of **somebody**. Whether it's one person in a job interview, or throngs of thousands in an auditorium, the ability to speak confidently is the same.

You can either fear speaking and try to avoid being noticed, or...

BAD!

you can embrace your natural abilities and learn to have fun with it.
The ability to speak confidently in all situations will help you develop relationships, excel in school, advance your career, and lead your family.

GOOD!

And if you think you can avoid speaking by **not** choosing obvious career paths such as actor, teacher, politician, or talk show host, it's not that easy. Think about these situations.

I've done it! If I don't speak, I am invisible!

- In school, you'll need to give book reports, maybe take part in a class debate, or just answer verbal questions.

- College will require entrance interviews, class interviews, and students are even providing video interviews now.

- Want a job? You'll have to do job interviews and then promotion interviews to advance.

- Write a book and the publisher will want you to tour.

- Become a mad scientist so you can hide away in a lab – you'll still need to present ideas and interview for grants.

- Many stay-at-home Moms get involved in community and education activities that involve speaking.

And on-and-on; the list is endless. Speaking cannot be avoided entirely. Nor should it be. By learning this skill, **you will open many doors and broaden your horizons far beyond what you thought possible.**

1.4 "WON'T THIS BE EMBARRASSING?"

It *could* be... if you let it. **Or** you could just have a lot of fun with it. For some people, embarrassment is very real and stops them from doing things they'd love to do. The good news? **Embarrassment is not fatal.**

In fact, most (if not all) of your audience will never notice it. No matter how visible you think your embarrassment is, **you** are much more aware of it than the people watching. Even if they should notice a little, they won't hold it against you. **You were willing to get up there and do this,** even though you were embarrassed. They will respect you for that.

"But, what if I'm nervous or anxious? I feel like I'm shaking."

Can they tell I'm nervous?

More good news! If you feel like your palms are sweating and your heart is pounding, your audience won't even notice. Just keep plugging away and make it fun. **Your audience will be listening to your words, not watching to see if your hands sweat.**

If you feel like you're nervous, shaking, sweaty, etc., you'll be surprised to find that **your audience was impressed by how calm and self-assured you looked.** Videotape your speech and you'll see that the nervousness barely shows.

One other thing... **don't mention or call attention to your embarrassment or nervousness.** Why point it out if most people aren't going to notice anyway? If you say something like, *"Please excuse my nervousness,"* then people are going to be looking for signs of that instead of listening to you. Just keep quiet and let people come to their own conclusions.

1.5 "WHAT IF I MESS UP?"

Even the greatest speakers "mess up" from time-to-time. They just ignore it and keep going. Most of the time, their audience doesn't even notice. If you make a mistake, you should NOT point it out, call attention to it, or apologize. What you consider a "mess up," **most people won't even notice.** If it's a big mistake, just smile, shrug, and keep going. Only correct it if it's necessary to correct misinformation.

Remember, **the audience does <u>not</u> know what you "planned to say."** They only know what you actually <u>did</u> say.

Now, if the mess up was so fundamentally wrong that it changes your message; provides false or misleading information; or otherwise **needs** to be corrected, just quickly make the correction and move on.

Here's a strange lesson: "**Never Expect Perfection!**"

Giving a speech should <u>not</u> be viewed as a staged act, but more as <u>an act of communication</u>. You will not be judged for the perfection of every single word, phrase, or movement. It's not like making a movie where you will do 50 takes until it's absolutely perfect.

Public speaking, presentations, interviews, etc. are about <u>sharing</u> a message and <u>connecting</u> with your audience. Your mission is to provide a well thought-out speech that expresses your ideas clearly and helps the audience understand your message. Entertainment can certainly be a part of that, but remember that it is ultimately about communication, not a faultless performance.

Once you realize **you do NOT have to be "perfect,"** you can begin to relax and enjoy yourself much more.

1.6   A Few Tips and Suggestions from Us

Here are a few tips, tidbits, and other bits of wisdom before we got started so you can get a jumpstart on being a great speaker. As we learn from our mistakes, **we also try to learn from the mistakes of others.** These tips are intended to help you get the most out of Gabberz and build a tool chest of powerful speaking tools. Please don't skip this section.

Okay, maybe that wasn't exactly the truth...

1.6.1   Ethics & Honesty

The old saying goes, "**A man is only as good as his word.**" Honesty, honor, faith, faithfulness... these are all characteristics people look for in one another. As a speaker, your audience will be looking for that from you. **They <u>want</u> to believe you; they want to believe <u>in</u> you.** Don't

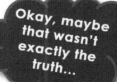

disappoint them. Don't give them reason to distrust you. Some examples of dishonesty in speeches include:

- providing quotes out of context;

- not providing details that would conflict with your point of view;

- holding back information to make your point is stronger than it is;

- giving non-typical or rare examples as proof;

- making it seem as if partial results are firm conclusions; or

- failing to attribute quotes or facts to the correct sources.

Honesty and ethical behavior should be a firm foundation in your life to begin with, but as we start moving into actual prepared speeches, the need to be aware of the honesty of your speeches becomes more evident. Because this topic is so important, we will be stressing **honesty, honor, faith,** and **faithfulness** to your audience throughout the program.

1.6.2 PLAGIARISM

Plagiarism [**pley**-j*uh*-riz-*uh*m] means to represent someone else's ideas, words, or work as your own. This doesn't *just* mean copying someone else's entire work word-for-word. It could mean copying quotations or pieces from single or multiple sources to build your work without giving proper credit to the original writers.

Of course, in preparing any writing, you'll do research, study, read the works of others—you'd be pretty boring if you didn't. However, you should never copy what others have done, but **you should create something new, something built from your own mind, with your own thoughts, your own interpretations, your own... flavor.** By 'adding' something new to the conversation, you make it your own.

> **No man has a good enough memory to make a successful liar.**
> *Abraham Lincoln*
> *(Which is a good thing, as the last thing we need is a successful liar!)*

1.6.3   NO NAME CALLING OR PERSONAL ATTACKS

There is **no need throughout Gabberz to ever call someone names or make personal attacks.** When a writer, speaker, or debater resorts to personal attacks, it generally means they have no factual basis for their discussion (or they're *just plain mean*). Provide the facts, your opinions, and/or your conclusions – leave personal attacks for those with less skill and experience than you.

1.6.4   SCRIBBLING BOOK

Start keeping a "**Scribbling Book**" or "**Idea Book**". Many people keep a little notebook handy they can stick in their pocket to capture thoughts, events, and references for little tidbits of life they think might make a good speech. We are strong believers in capturing these little tidbits of life. **These great ideas are fleeting, passing by quickly, unlikely to be thought of again, so capture them while you can.**

Keeping a list of all these little thoughts and ideas will help you tremendously as you get to lessons where you have to write speeches for yourself. You'd be surprised at how often these thoughts begin to occur to you when you start paying attention. Like any skill, you need to practice this until it becomes automatic.

1.6.5   VIDEOTAPE YOUR SPEECHES

You should **videotape your speeches**, then review them carefully. Besides being fun to watch, these recordings will help you focus on the lessons and watch for improvement. If you were nervous or scared, you probably won't see that on the tape. Neither did your audience. You will also have the option of getting a **professional analysis by Gabberz Coaches**, visit www.gabberz.com for more information.

1.6.6   KEEP YOUR BUTTERFLIES IN FORMATION

You've probably heard the expression, "**butterflies in your stomach.**" You may even have experienced it. This is a common expression, and a common feeling among some people.

Some coaches will try to get their students to do mental tricks to get the butterflies to go away. We think it is better for you to **control them and harness your nervous energy than to try to make them go away through mental gymnastics** like trying to imagine your audience in their underwear to distract you from your natural condition.

Fear is okay. Nervousness is okay. These are known factors you can learn to be comfortable with. By **forcing the butterflies to fly in formation** at your command, you can use that energy to make your speech more energetic and engaging.

1.6.7 DON'T BE A MEANDERTHAL

This is one of our favorites. Although the general usage of the term "**meander*thal***" applies to someone who wanders aimlessly, blocking the path of others, we like to use the term in relation to public speaking.

We define a **Meanderthal** as "*someone who has difficulty communicating crisply and is prone to giving long, unfocused speeches.*" You know, the kind of speeches that put people to sleep. A Meanderthal will write their speech without giving thought to flow, pacing, or their audience, and will just meander aimlessly, following their stream of consciousness wherever it takes them.

Your speech should have a point. It should be expressed in logical order, building point-by-point, until your listeners arrive at the conclusion with you.

1.6.8 MAKE SURE THE JOKE'S NOT ON YOU

You'll sometimes get advice from others to warm up your audience and start your speech with a joke. This can "sometimes" be effective, but is **not at all necessary**.

The risk you run is your joke flopping right at the outset when the audience has not yet had a chance to form an opinion of your speech. The only way this can be effective is **if the joke is a good one AND is appropriate for the audience**. Save the jokes until you have significant experience and can read your audience well. Humor will be a part of many of the lessons throughout the program, but you'll learn methods to be funny and entertaining without resorting to bad jokes.

1.6.9 DON'T LEARN IT WORD-FOR-WORD

Know your material very well, but don't over-rehearse to the point where you are just reciting your speech. You should **rarely memorize your speech** and deliver it word-for-word. There are times to do that, but we'll discuss those later.

Speaking word-for-word what you've written down may make your speech sound canned. Your audience will notice. **They'll be much more receptive if you're speaking from knowledge or from the heart.** Write your speech similar to how you talk, not in a formal written narrative. You always want to **talk with** your audience, not recite them a book.

1.6.10 BODY LANGUAGE

We'll be working a lot on body language throughout the program. We'll go from one extreme to the other, all aimed at just making you comfortable in your own body in front of other people. **Depending on the study and the source, it is said that more than 50% of the message that we deliver to people is through our body language: our facial expressions, how we stand/sit, what we do with our hands, etc.** We have some fun exercises in the program where you will force your body language to tell a different story than your words. It's interesting to see what happens when your words don't match your body language.

1.6.11 PEOPLE WANT YOU TO SUCCEED

With rare exception, **people want you to succeed**. They are attending your speech to support you and they'd also like to be entertained, stimulated, and informed. **They get what they want through *your* success, so focus on the fact that <u>you are not alone</u>, the audience is your partner in this affair.** Seek their support, their guidance, and interact with them. Whenever you engage with your audience—even if it's only an audience of one—everyone comes out a winner.

1.6.12 VISUALIZE YOURSELF GIVING THE SPEECH

While practicing for your speech, don't just rehearse the words, **visualize yourself speaking to your audience** in the location where you will do this. Imagine your voice is clear, loud, self-assured.

Always maintain a positive frame of mind where you see yourself succeeding, instead of imagining all the things that could go wrong. **Try this...** Imagine one of the great athletes you know of. When they are practicing, do you think they imagine *missing* the shot? Or do you think they visualize themselves making the shot and celebrating the win? **<u>They will visualize the win of course</u>**. That's how they become winners. You should do the same!

If possible, do some of your practices in the room you will be speaking in with a pretend audience made up of pillows, stuffed animals, or your dog. Speak to them as you would your live audience. Visualize. Imagine. See their faces. **Convince yourself you will be successful.**

1.6.13 GAIN MORE EXPERIENCE

Gabberz is designed to provide you many opportunities to speak in front of people. You'll get the most out of this program if you seek out other opportunities to speak *beyond* what's scheduled in the program.

Plan a toast for a family gathering, or even just for the family dinner. Look for opportunities at school; at organizations you belong to such as the Boy Scouts or Girl Scouts; see if you can speak at your Mother's book club meeting. Opportunities abound if you're willing to look for them.

You don't need to do this in the beginning (or ever), but as you gain more experience and confidence, **you may be looking for more and more opportunities to hone your skills**. And once you find the joy of speaking, opportunities will present themselves throughout your life—it's your choice whether you take advantage of them or not.

1.6.14 MOST OF ALL... RELAX AND HAVE FUN !

I gotta be me!

One of the main points we stress throughout the **Gabberz** program is to relax and have fun with it. It shouldn't be stressful or create anxiety. **Move at your own pace, prepare for each lesson, and concentrate on giving your audience a joyful experience**.

It's important that you be true to yourself, both on and off "stage". When you stand up to speak, **you should give your speech as "You"**, and not try to force yourself into some imagined image (we will make an exception to this rule during certain lessons). Relax and be yourself, it will be easier for you, and your audience will appreciate your faithfulness to your own character.

We'll cover this in more detail later, but your lessons will not be scored so much on technical correctness (especially in the beginning), but on **how hard you try and the passion you put into the effort**.

1.7 MULTIPLE STUDENTS IN A HOUSEHOLD

This program can easily be used by multiple students in a family. In fact, **the more the merrier**. Just remember to purchase a book for each student so they can take notes and refer to information later. Larger families mean larger audiences and more interaction during the exercises. Additionally, this means several students will

be doing similar exercises and you can learn from each other. However, having multiple students doing the program can also be challenging, so there are a few things to be aware of:

- **Be Courteous and Attentive**: when you are playing the part of audience member, you should give the speaker all of your attention and respect, just as you would like to receive as the speaker.

- **No Guided Missiles**: "Guided Missiles" are simply interrupting someone to say "no", to object, to make an absolute negative declaration without letting the speaker finish or without considering all of the information first. Don't do it!

- **Same or Different**: Siblings may be in different age groups, or at different levels, so they will be doing different lessons. In that case, you should still schedule everyone to give their speeches at the same time so that you get the whole family together and you build on each other's energy. If you are in the same age group at the same level, you can do the same lessons, but take turns on who goes first.

> Be not afraid of going slowly; be afraid only of standing still.
>
> *Chinese Proverb*
>
> *(Don't get caught up in the instructions or doing things "just right". In Level 1, you __cannot__ do the speech wrong, as long as you just get up and do it.)*

www.gabberz.com

Public Speaking for Kids, Tweens, and Teens

Level 1, Single-Student, Do-it-Yourself

CHAPTER 2

HOW TO USE THIS GUIDE

What You'll Learn in This Chapter:

✓ How do I prepare?

✓ What role does my family play?

✓ How do I schedule events?

✓ How does an exercise/lesson work – what happens?

2   HOW TO USE THIS GUIDE

2.1   INTRODUCTION

Our goal is to make **Gabberz** as simple and fun as possible so that you can enjoy the program, rather than trying to figure out how to do it. **Every lesson in this program is laid out the same way** so that once you figure out how to do Lesson 1, you can rest easy that you'll be able to figure out Lesson 6, Lesson 10, and so on.

Each lesson is laid out like this (with a <u>few minor exceptions</u>):

> **TIP:**
>
> *You can use these wide margins to write notes to help you remember important points.*

- **Section 1: Overview**

  The Overview provides tells you what's going to happen in that particular lesson. It will provide you with expectations, goals, and a big-picture look at what you'll need to do to complete the lesson.

- **Section 2: Prepare**

  This section gives you step-by-step instructions for how to prepare for this lesson. Here, you'll find out if you'll be reading a Gabberz-provided speech, writing your own, or doing something entirely different.

- **Section 3: Practice**

  Guidance on the best way to practice for that particular lesson. Some lessons will require a fair bit of practice, others none at all. In each case, we'll give you instructions on the best way to reach your goal.

- **Section 4: Present**

  This will be important tips, hints, and guidance for how to get the most of each lesson. This section also includes a very important "**Do/Do Not**" table. This will give you an easy reference for what you should or should not be doing during your speech.

  Understanding how the lessons are laid out is important!

- **Section 5: Speech Time**

  Finally, we get to the fun part. Here's where we get into how you do the exercises and speeches. You'll get **step-by-step instructions** for each exercise and/or speech; how to prepare your audience; preparation of your "auditorium" (probably your living room); and any other information you need to succeed. This section will also include an "Analysis and Scoring" section **Remember though, you cannot do any lesson in Level 1 wrong, as long as you do it.**

- **Section 6:** **Congratulations!** **Prepare for the Next Lesson.**

The last section in each lesson will give you a very simple introduction to what you will be doing in the next lesson. Most importantly though, it will give you instructions for preparing your audience for your next speech **while you still have them in the room from *this* speech**. For example, in most cases, you'll want to get everyone to commit to a day and time for your next speech so they can get it on their calendar and you'll know exactly how much time you'll have to prepare

That's it! **Each lesson will be fully contained and organized** basically the same way so that you don't have to worry about figuring out the process. **Easy!**

If you do find yourself getting lost, confused, or frustrated – **don't panic!** There are a few simple things you can do to get back on track.

1. **Stop**. Take a deep breath. And relax, knowing that you'll soon be back on track.

2. Go back and **re-read** the lesson, taking good notes of the important points in the wide white space provided to the left or right of each page.

3. Come back and **re-read** this chapter, "How to Use This Guide."

4. **Ask your parents** to help you get started on the lesson and provide guidance. Everyone wants you to succeed and should be happy to help.

5. If you're still having problems, **just get up there and do it** however you think it should be done. The next lesson will come easier.

We cannot succeed if you do not succeed! If you are having problems understanding the material, find it confusing, or if you just see a better way to do something, **let us know**. We are always trying to improve the program and would love to hear any suggestions from you. Just pop over to our website at **www.gabberz.com** and send a message through our **Contact Us** page.

2.2 THE "LET'S GET STARTED" SPEECH (CHAPTER 4)

The structured lessons will start in Chapter 5, however, we start you out with a very easy speech in Chapter 4 that we've already written for you. Chapter 4 is one of those exceptions and is structured a little differently than defined above. There is a lot of material we'd like to introduce you to before you get into the heart of the lessons and we want to give you a very easy speech to start with to get your feet wet.

In **Chapter 4**, we will cover the basics to get you going:

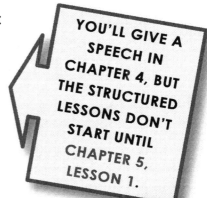

- All about public speaking

- Parent/family support

- Your preparation

- Nervousness and fear

- Review and scoring

All of this ends up with your first speech which will essentially be reading a speech prepared by Gabberz. Like we said, **easy!**

2.3 SUPPORT

Your parents or instructor should provide varying degrees of support and help depending on the lessons and your age. Although the program is designed so that you can do all the lessons on your own, always seek your help and support if you need it.

2.4 PLANNING AND SCHEDULING

You should always try to make the speech portion of your lesson an "event". Plan it, schedule it, make sure you have the right tools and props ready, and **get as large an audience as you're comfortable with**. If you make this an event, you will be more excited and your audience will be more engaged. You might even want to enlist someone to introduce you each time.

Generally, each lesson is designed for one to two weeks. If you believe you need longer to prepare, that's okay. But you don't want to let too much time go between your lessons or you'll lose your momentum and

find yourself forgetting important points. If you want to go faster, that's okay too. Just be sure you're getting the most out of each lesson.

Schedule your next "event" while you have everyone in the room at your current "event". You will have a deadline and everyone can put the event on their schedules. Be sure to remind them of the date later

2.5 SPEECH TIME

Some lessons use Gabberz-provided speeches. Other lessons will require you to write the speech (later, we'll spend time on coming up with topics; that's easy once you get the hang of it). And then there are some lessons that you just can't prepare for. **You'll have to learn to be fast on your feet** to make the most of those.

2.6 ANALYSIS & SCORING

Analysis and scoring of your speeches concentrate on **your effort and your passion** – _not_ your technical correctness. Although we do look to improve your technical skills over time, perfection is not expected, especially in the beginning.

No doubt, some of your audience members will offer well-meaning advice from time-to-time. **Some of that advice may be helpful, some may not**. They mean well, they want to help, but they may not understand the step-by-step nature of what we're doing here.

Take all advice graciously, happily, and without disagreement. You may put it in the back of your mind if you like, but if it's not consistent with what you've already learned, it may be way too early for that type of advice, or it could be completely contrary to what we are teaching.

2.7 THE LAST MINUTE

Don't do it. **Don't wait until the last minute.** It's not fair to you or your audience. If they're willing to come to your event, **the least you can do is give them your best**. Every time!

www.gabberz.com

Public Speaking for Kids, Tweens, and Teens
Level 1, Single-Student, Do-it-Yourself

CHAPTER 3

TOOLS & TECHNIQUES

What You'll Learn in This Chapter:

✓ How to find topics for the speeches you need to write.

✓ How to build a backlog of ideas.

✓ What to do if your mind goes blank.

3   TOOLS & TECHNIQUES

3.1   INTRODUCTION

The **Gabberz** program is designed to provide you all the tools you need to be successful. Remember, **Gabberz** is about about building self-confidence and being comfortable just being you.

3.2   TOOLS

Each guide includes everything you need in order to complete that level. Your package might include:

- **Gabberz-Prepared Speeches**

  Some of the lessons require that you use a speech prepared by **Gabberz** rather than write your own. The provided speeches are in the back of this book in Appendices. The lesson will tell you when to use the speech and how to use it. The content in all speeches are appropriate for all age groups.

- **Scoring/Analysis Tools**

  The lessons include scoring/analysis sheets for you and your audience to use to help you gauge your success at meeting the goals of that lesson. When your speech event is over, pass the book around and ask your audience to score the audience sheet. You can fill out your score sheet. Remember, you cannot do the lessons wrong. The scores are only for your information to see where you can improve.

- **Other Materials**

We are always seeking ways to improve or enhance the program (**your suggestions are always welcome!**). Be sure to register your manual on www.gabberz.com so we can let you know whenever anything new is available.

It is important that you keep this training guidebook where you can find it when needed, and that you follow the rules designed for each lesson. Doing so will help you get the most out of this program, and **ensure you have the most fun**.

3.3 TRAINING METHODS

Each lesson contains everything you need to know in order to successfully meet your goals for that lesson. All methods are designed to reinforce important elements of speech, voice, body language, personal/group interaction, organization, and the other tools you'll need to develop self-confidence and a joy in speaking to others.

Not to mention, the lessons are just plain fun. You'll act, move, yell, cry, surprise your audience, and stretch yourself to do new and exciting things. You may wonder sometimes **why** you have to do some of this stuff. Trust us, there's a method to our madness. But, sometimes, it's all just good fun.

3.4 TOPICS—WHAT WILL I TALK ABOUT?

3.4.1 TOPICS—PICKING IS HARD TO DO

For some people, finding a topic to speak about is harder than giving the speech. For others, the hard part is picking one topic from the long list of things they want to talk about. If you think it will be hard to come up with a topic, there's good news!

Once you learn how to recognize ideas that are all around you, your head will spin with the possibilities!

We'll provide you with some easy steps right now. Later, we'll provide you some tips so you'll never run short of ideas.

3.4.2 TOPICS—REMEMBER THE SCRIBBLING BOOK?

Remember the little notebook we talked about earlier. **This is where it's really important.** Once you train your mind to recognize opportunities, possibilities, thoughts, events, and words that have potential, you have to have some place to capture them. Otherwise, **in the rush of life, they just pass on by, possibly never to return.**

Keep something handy to write these things down. My pockets are always stuffed with notes, Post-its®, napkins, and other things with scribbled notes on them. Of course, a smart phone could be handy too.

3.4.3 TOPICS—WHAT DO YOU KNOW?

The easiest way to start your list is to **make a list of the things you know**. You'd be surprised at how much knowledge you have on many topics. Think it's all boring, mundane stuff nobody would like to hear about? **Think again.**

Start with the stuff you have a passion for. Your passion and excitement will come through while you are speaking and will energize your audience. Don't just recite facts and statistics, **find a story to tell**. Add your "flavor" to it, make it yours. Make us care about it.

Is your passion Football? Don't give statistics to convince us who's going to win the Super Bowl. Give us a story about your passion to lead a Major League team, driving the ball during the last 30 seconds down the final 20 yards to victory.

Whether you know it or not, you know a lot of things. First, **get out your Scribbling Book (or your smart phone)**. Now, start making a list of the things you know. No matter how silly, boring, or inconsequential you think something might be, **put it all down**.

- Are you into sports? Music? Reading?

- How about old TV shows?

- Do you build model cars or airplanes?

- Have you studied all the skateboarding moves?

- Do you collect American Girl® dolls, stamps, limited edition baseball cards, classic comics, etc.?

- Have you studied dinosaurs? Or Greek Mythology?

- Maybe you like cooking?

Look around your room. Look around the house. Look at your family. It doesn't matter if you think the topic might be boring, simple, uninteresting, or that nobody else will have an interest in it. You haven't come up with a story yet, **you're just putting together a list**. You don't have to have details at this point. All you need is a list.

Make an inventory of what you know. The ideas for your speech will come later.

Even if you believe you are "only you"—that your life is uninteresting, boring, or just plain ordinary—the truth and the exciting part is that **you are unique. There's only one of you in the world!** It's your perspective, your thoughts, your... flavor that will make what you speak about interesting. Remember, anyone can give us facts, only you can give us what makes you unique.

But don't worry about how to do that right now. We'll work on that throughout the course and by the end of it all **you'll be wondering how you're going to find all the speaking opportunities you need to even make a dent in your list of things to talk about.**

3.4.4 TOPICS—WHAT DO YOU _WANT_ TO KNOW?

The next easiest part of your list is to think about the things that you always *wanted* to know more about. Famous people, rare animals, deep water sharks, foreign lands, planting rutabagas, animation, whatever it might be. What better time to learn about these things than in the preparation of a speech?

Here's my prediction... **Once you have some of these lists going, and you see how much there is that you already know, it won't be so daunting, and the ideas for turning these into stories for your speeches will start to come to you.** Don't worry if they don't at first, we'll help you out along the way.

3.4.5 TOPICS—HOW ABOUT THINGS YOU'VE DONE?

This one's easy once you start thinking about it. What have you done during your life? Where have you been? What activities have you been involved in. Here are a few thoughts for you:

- Where have you gone on your last 3 vacations?

- Have you been to a foreign country?

- Have you gone to weddings? Graduations? Funerals?

- Birthday parties? Did they do anything unusual?

- What movies have you been to? Theater? Drive-in?

- Have you been to political rallies? Protests?

- Have you been on an airplane? Train? Ship?

- Have you been to the beach? (The shark wants to know.)

- Classic car show? Boat show? Convention?

- Have you visited your Father's workplace?

You see, once you start thinking about it, you've done a lot of stuff, been a lot of places, seen things of interest. Bet your lists are starting to get pretty long about now. Maybe some speech ideas are starting to pop into your head. **Be sure to write those story ideas down also.** You can put the story ideas on new pages, or jot them down next to the topic that sparked your interest.

Maybe you're thinking might go something like this:

1. You look through your list and "**movie**" catches your eye.

2. You've seen some okay movies, but you're not really excited about doing a movie review. Yawnnnnn...

3. So you think, "**What else could I talk about?**" The concession stand? Maybe. The candy? The seats? The theater itself? People talking during the movie? Maybe.

4. Then **you remember going to the Drive-In last summer**. You had a great time so you start thinking about that.

5. What was interesting or different? Some thoughts come to mind.

   a. It was hot; you got kind of sweaty, but didn't care.

   b. The popcorn was super buttery and the pizza was great.

   c. You sprawled out in the grass, watching the movie and sipping on a giant diet soda. All was grand.

6. A story about how great the drive-in was would be okay. **But then you start to remember something else**.

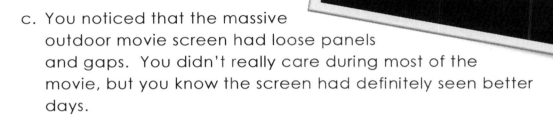

   a. You remember your parents talking about how drive-ins used to be all over the place, but this was the last one in the area. Very few are left.

   b. You remember the playground equipment you enjoyed was old and in a little disrepair.

   c. You noticed that the massive outdoor movie screen had loose panels and gaps. You didn't really care during most of the movie, but you know the screen had definitely seen better days.

7. You start to wonder why the drive-in struggles to survive. You enjoyed it so much, why have they disappeared? **This is where the "you" part comes in and you make this your own story**. Maybe your speech now becomes:

   ✓ "An American Icon—Vanishing Before Our Eyes?"

   ✓ "The Drive-In has All But Disappeared—I Say It's About Time."

   ✓ "Can We Save the Drive-In?"

   ✓ "Should We Save the Drive-In or Let it Die?"

   ✓ "We Went To The Drive-In and Had a Great Time—But It Made Me Sad."

   ✓ "It Was Hot, It Was Buggy, and I'm Still in Pain from Falling in the Gravel under the Swingset—but I'll Remember It as One of the Best Times of My Childhood."

   ✓ "The Drive-In—It's Not About the Movie at All, It's About the Experience."

8. Or maybe it becomes something entirely different.

Public Speaking for Kids, Tweens, and Teens – Confidence for Life!

Do you see now how your thoughts might have led you down a path to create something that has *your* flavor? **You've made it something unique, just like you.** What's really grand though is that, if you did this exercise yourself and started with "movie", you would have ended up someplace entirely different. And in a place just as grand—maybe even more so.

3.4.6   TOPICS—DO YOU HAVE OPINIONS?

Are you starting to see how this works now? You should have a long list of things in your list by now, and maybe a bunch of story ideas. If not, don't worry about it. You have plenty of time before you have to write your first speech.

Okay, time to make another list

Do you have an opinion? Sure you do. You probably have many. Now is the time to start listing your beliefs, opinions, thoughts, values, and other things that are "you". Keep in mind that **these don't all have to be big political opinions.** They could simply be the category of music you like or the color of your team's jersey. **Big or small, capture it all.**

- Social, political, and societal issues

- School policies, events, and news

- Homeschools, Private Schools, Charter Schools

- Current events

- Use of social media (Facebook, Twitter, etc.)

- Religion, God, Evangelism

- Skateboards vs. blades, vs. bikes

- Types of music you hate (or love)

- Types of books you love (or hate)

- Talking/texting while driving

Think about what you talk about around the dinner table. Or what you argue with your friends about. **Once you start writing these down, you'll find that you have a lot of opinions.**

3.4.7 TOPICS—WRAPPING UP—FOR NOW

We've covered a lot of material on how to come up with topics for your speeches. Hopefully, you've come up with some strong lists and possibly some good story ideas. Either way, we'll be working on this more. In the meantime, here are some other methods you can use to expand your lists:

- **Random Searches (Dictionary, Encyclopedia, Internet)**

  Simply thumb through some of these for anything that catches your eye. You may or may not have any knowledge of the topic, but it doesn't matter, you're just getting a list of topics and ideas.

- **Brainstorming (don't worry, it won't hurt)**

  There are many ways to do brainstorming, either alone or with help from others. You simply pick a topic or a group of items from a topic and try to come up with as many ideas as you can, as quickly as you can. They can be silly, stupid, unrealistic, even fanciful. The purpose is just to get the brain juices flowing and get a bunch of stuff down on paper. From that, sometimes inspiration is born.

- **Free Association (let your mind run wild)**

  Free association is similar to brainstorming, but you don't really stick with a topic. You just let your mind wander and follow whatever path it takes from your starting point. You pick a word, write down whatever word occurs to you first from that one, then write down whatever occurs to you from the second word, etc.

  Keep writing down the very first thing that occurs to you, no matter how far away it is from your original topic. Just sit back and let your mind lead the way. **Don't try to outguess yourself.** You might be surprised where you end up.

The point of all this is just to relax, build your lists, and train yourself to watch for the stories to come to you. **Imagine all the possibilities**... and we haven't even talked yet about just watching the world around you.

www.gabberz.com

Public Speaking for Kids, Tweens, and Teens
Level 1, Single-Student, Do-it-Yourself

CHAPTER 4

LET'S GET STARTED—SPEECH TIME

What You'll Learn in This Chapter:

✓ Prepare for your first speech.

✓ Everything about what you and your audience need to do.

✓ Schedule an actual event.

✓ Score this lesson.

Public Speaking for Kids, Tweens, and Teens – Confidence for Life!

4   LET'S GET STARTED—SPEECH TIME

4.1   INTRODUCTION

Yay! It's time for your first speech. Don't worry; we'll make it painless and fun. **You might even surprise yourself.**

This first **Introductory Speech** and this section are a little different from the lessons starting in Chapter 5. We need to do a little housekeeping and introduce you to some concepts and tools.

The first tool we're going to introduce you to is the **Quick Look Table**. This table will be in the introduction of every lesson and will give you all the requirements for that lesson.

LESSON QUICK LOOK – Introductory Speech	
Prep. Time	**1 Week**
Schedule	Date _____ Day _____ Time _____
Exercise	If an exercise is required, it will be listed here.
Lesson	3 minute speech (read provided speech twice).
Speech	Gabberz-provided speech **Appendix A— Introductory Speech**. Follow the instructions for use of the speech. **Do not memorize the speech word-for-word.** Just get comfortable reading it and follow instructions.
Goals	The goal for this lesson is just to get up and give a speech in front of your audience. You don't have to be good, you don't have to be perfect, **you can even mess up a bunch**. All that's required is for you to just get up and do it.

This is how much time you should give yourself to prepare for your speech "event".

Get a commitment from your audience as soon as possible. Enter the scheduled date and time here.

Do you need to write a speech? Or read one provided by Gabberz?

Goals for this lesson.

More detail and instructions will be provided in the sections that follow in exactly the order we laid out for you previously in Section 2.1.

Although we recommend you read the entire lesson before starting your preparations, **you should <u>go ahead right now and schedule your event</u> with your audience.** The sooner you get that done, the easier it will be for you to plan for your "event".

Remember that **this section will be a little different** from all the lessons starting with Lesson 1 in Chapter 5. Before we get into the introductory speech you'll be doing here, we want to give you a little more information about Public Speaking. **Relax and enjoy the information, you _don't_ have to memorize it.**

4.2   ABOUT PUBLIC SPEAKING

Although the concentration of this course is "Public Speaking", **the skills you learn here will help you build confidence in many different aspects of life.** Once you are secure in your ability to speak in front of other people, you'll have more confidence to express yourself in groups, at gatherings, in front of the classroom, or even at the dinner table. Here are a few things you should know about public speaking.

4.2.1   BE AN EFFECTIVE LISTENER

Being an effective Public Speaker is also about learning to listen. Learn to be an effective listener and you can engage with people rather than talking at them.

4.2.2   THREE MAIN GOALS OF PUBLIC SPEAKING

There can be many reasons for public speaking, or speaking in general, but these can generally be broken down into three primary goals:

- To **inform/instruct** people about things they don't know;

- To **persuade** people to believe or do something; or

- To **entertain** people.

Notice that all three goals are directed at "**people**". You must always remember that the focus of your speech or discussion should be on your audience. **Without them, you're just talking to yourself.**

Often, all three goals are combined, but a good speech has one of these as the **primary goal** and is written for your intended audience.

No matter your goal, you will rely on similar skills: you'll use feedback to adapt your message to the audience; you'll use stories or metaphors to help the audience understand your message; and you'll organize your thoughts logically with messages tailored for your audience.

4.2.3 VALIDATION

Never try to trick your audience into accepting your idea or argument by providing false, misleading, or partial information. Let your audience make their own determination from the **valid information you've given them**. They will agree, or not. If everybody agreed on everything, this would be a pretty boring world.

Your word and your reputation are some of the most valuable things you own—protect them with all your might. Once your reputation becomes tainted by trying to trick or mislead your audience, it will be hard to earn back that lost trust.

- Get your facts from multiple reliable sources.

- **Validate your sources.** The Internet is notorious for spreading misinformation, lies, or mistakes.

- Keep good notes and record your sources.

- **Do not exaggerate, embellish beyond the truth, or otherwise insult your audience's intelligence** by trying to make your point by talking over their heads.

- Finally, **be prepared to answer questions about your topic**.

4.3 FEEL THE WIND IN YOUR FACE

Number one rule... have fun! Many people with a fear of speaking are envious of those who enjoy it and do it well. What they don't realize is that public speaking is really no different than riding a bike.

At first, you're a little hesitant, concerned that you will fall, that you'll get hurt. But **if you're willing to give it a try, you can learn to do it well**. At first, you might be wobbly, shaky, a little unsure of yourself. But you keep at it and start to gain a little confidence. Before you know it, you're zipping around, pushing the envelope, **feeling the wind in your face**. Enjoying yourself.

It's the same with public speaking. You might be a little shaky at first. You might be a

little unsure how it's going to go. Worried that you might crash and get embarrassed. But with practice, **you'll soon feel the wind in your face** and wonder why you were ever concerned. **You'll find the joy of speaking** and you'll seek out opportunities to do it over and over again.

4.4 PERFECTION IS OVERRATED

There are a few things in life where you need to be perfect, or near-perfect. Public speaking is **not** one of them. If you spend your time worrying about being perfect—practicing over and over till every word follows every other word perfectly—you'll just end up sounding stilted, over-practiced, and it will sound like you're reading a script. **Awful!**

Of course, **you must always do your best!** You should work hard at structuring your material properly, researching it, preparing it, learning it, and practicing it. But you should not practice delivery to perfection.

Very rarely is a good speech given in exactly the same way with the same words every time it is given. **Good speakers know their material!** They don't memorize the speech word-for-word. They learn their material and the outline and key points they want to address—then they talk with their audience using the knowledge they have of the subject matter. **This is how they let their passion come out.** Reading a script does not let them express what they feel.

Yes, you might miss a point here and there. You might even get something wrong occasionally. But, the audience will enjoy your speech much more. Remember... *the audience does not know what you were going to say, they only know what you did say*!

Work hard, always do your best, and no matter what happens, it will be "perfect" enough.

IMPORTANT POINT !

Finally !

It's time to prepare for your first speech.

4.5 PREPARE

4.5.1 OVERVIEW

All of the lessons in the Gabberz program will be structured on what we call the three "P's" of giving a speech:

- **Prepare**: this is where we tell you what you'll need to do for the lesson and how you'll prepare for your speech event.

- **Practice**: the practice section will give you instructions and tips on how to practice. In some cases, we won't want you to practice. Those are even more fun!

- **Present**: this section will provide you with tips for giving your speech and getting the most out of your goals. This will also include a "**Do/Do Not Table**" with lists of things you should or should not do during your speech.

4.5.2 PREPARE FOR YOUR INTRODUCTORY SPEECH

This "Introductory Speech" is designed for **two main goals**.

1. **Get you in front of an audience** with an easy speech so you can experience an actual speech event and begin the process of "riding this bike".

2. **Give a "baseline" speech** so you can see how you improve over time. **We HIGHLY recommend that you <u>videotape</u> this introductory speech** so you can go back and review it later. To get the most out of this lesson, **you should videotape this speech, then tape it again after you complete the program**. Compare the recordings and you'll see the incredible difference in your confidence, presentation, and abilities.

> COME BACK HERE AFTER READING THE ENTIRE CHAPTER.

> I love watching the tapes of my speeches!

Public Speaking for Kids, Tweens, and Teens – Confidence for Life!

What You'll Be Doing – Introductory Speech

What	You'll read a **Gabberz-prepared speech.** You do not have to write anything for this lesson. • Your introductory speech is located in **Appendix A.**
When	Date _____ Day _____ Time _____ You should schedule this speech event for about **one week** after you start this lesson. This speech event will take <u>less than 10 minutes</u>. • If you have not already scheduled your speech event, **please do so now.**
Who	Try to schedule your speeches with **as many people for your audience as possible** (or you are comfortable with). • You can start with just your immediate family for an audience, but more people means more fun. • Start with parents, then brothers and sisters, then extended family (cousins, Aunts, Uncles, etc.), then reach out to friends and people you (and your family) know at church, Scouts, sports team, etc.
Where	You should always try to **make your speech an "Event".** • You and the audience will become much more engaged if you make this special, scheduled, and arranged. • Try to do this where you can set up arranged seating, maybe a makeshift podium of some kind, or even a handmade sign or lighting to set the mood. You don't have to go overboard, but make it fun and interesting. • If you can't set aside an area like that, the living room works well with the audience seated as if they're watching TV with you standing in front of the TV. • The dinner table can work well also. Just make sure the dishes are cleared away and you are standing in front of everyone. If possible, try to turn the chairs so no one is sitting at the table. Sitting at a table tends to distance people from you. Don't sit at the table yourself.

Prepare	The Gabberz-prepared speech can be reviewed now, but the speech should NOT be memorized.
	We would like you to be familiar with it and follow the instructions in the speech, but you should have the speech in your hands to refer to as much as needed. **This lesson is NOT about memorizing your speech.** This is one of the few times we'll ask you to read from a script during the speech.
	VERY IMPORTANT: This lesson is <u>NOT</u> about giving a great speech; it's **just** about getting up and doing it.
	Here are a few things you can do to prepare:
	• Study and practice your speech according to the practice section coming up.
	• Prepare for your speaking room and your event by creating any signs, tools, props, or anything else you would like to make the speech more exciting or fun.
	• Get someone to introduce you. You can even provide them with a short biography about you to read.
	• Remind your audience about the upcoming event (maybe prepare tickets or flyers to hand out in advance).

LESSON 0—EXERCISE

What?	Some lessons will require a complimentary exercise or activity along with the speech. This Introductory Speech does not require an additional exercise.

LESSON 0—INTRODUCTORY SPEECH

What?	Gabberz-provided **Introductory Speech in Appendix A**. You'll read this speech twice.
Length?	2 to 3 minute speech read at normal speaking speed. **Do not rush the speech.** During practice, time yourself.
Repeat during the event	1. Read the speech in front of your audience the first time. 2. Get audience reaction. 3. Reset and **give the speech a second time** to see if it feels any different to you. 4. If multiple students are speaking, alternate turns.
Subject?	This speech is a humorous adaptation of famous speeches throughout history.

4.6 PRACTICE

Okay, it's time to start feeling the wind in your face. By now, you should have scheduled your speech event and you should have about a week to go. More or less time is okay, just try not to let too much time pass between your speech events—**you want to keep the momentum going**.

The practice portion is not complicated for this one. **Here are a few tips, hints, and guidelines** to get you started.

- Understand the level of practice necessary for a speech. A casual, off-the-cuff speech about a topic you're very familiar with will take little practice. A technical speech aimed at instructing or coaching others will require more practice.

- Think about how closely you need to follow the material. Can you stray and embellish (as in an opinion piece)? Or do you need to stick closely to the prepared material (like a historical study)?

- Remember, you do **not** want to over-practice your speech so that you end up sounding like you're reciting a script. You want to know the material well enough to present it reasonably comfortably, but not memorized word-for-word.

PRACTICE YOUR INTRODUCTORY SPEECH

1. Bookmark or copy the **Introductory Speech in Appendix A**.

2. Read the instructions and the speech to yourself now.

Don't over-practice or this could happen! Just kidding!

3. **For this speech**, there are no strict rules on how closely you must follow instructions. If instructed to speak a part using an imitated voice or accent, do only what you're comfortable with. **You and your audience will enjoy it much more if you really take the instructions to heart and exaggerate the parts**, we leave that to you (please do it).

4. Practice the speech **out loud at full volume at least 10 times** between now and your speech event. You may practice more if you like, but don't overdo it.

5. If possible, **try to practice where others cannot hear you** such as in the basement or behind closed doors while they're watching TV. You will feel less self-conscious and you'd like your audience to hear your speech for the first time when at your event.

6. **Your practices should always be out loud**, given at the volume you intend to use when you give the speech.

There's NO wrong way to do this one as long as you get up and do it.

7. The speech should be **2 to 3 minutes long**. Time yourself as you practice and learn to use pacing and pauses for effect to provide impact. Be even more careful during your live speech that you **don't let nervousness make you speed up**. Concentrate on speaking at the speed you practiced at. If you go too fast the first time, make a conscious effort to slow it down the second time you give the speech.

8. At some point, you may get advice from someone to practice in front of a mirror. That's okay, but we don't think it's generally necessary. **We want you concentrating on the words and the sound of your voice**. When you become comfortable with those, your face will be fine.

9. If possible, try to do a couple of practices in the room where you will be holding your event.

10. For some speeches, you may prepare note cards or other tools to help you remember important points. Don't do any of that on this speech. Just use the text provided in this book. You may highlight some points if you like.

11. <u>Don't worry</u> **about all the rules, tips, suggestions, and other things we talked about** in previous chapters. We'll work on all of those throughout the lessons. Right now, you just want to relax and give your speech. **There is no wrong way to do this one as long as you get up there and do it.**

12. **Have fun!**

4.7 PRESENT

It's almost time for your speech event. A few notes before the big show.

1. A couple of days before your speech, verify that everyone remembers the event and still plans to attend.

2. If you have prepared any props, tools, or anything else that you'll use during the speech, verify that they are ready and work as you anticipate. Do a dry run or two if possible.

3. The day of the event, double-check to make sure you have everything you need, such as the copy of the speech.

Finally, each lesson will have a **Do/Do Not Table**. The table provides pointers for things to do or not do during the presentation to help meet your goals and provide a better experience for you and your audience.

DO/DO NOT TABLE Introductory Speech	
DO	**DO NOT**
• Smile and gesture. • Stand tall and straight. • Look your audience in the eye and talk to them. • **Keep going**, even if you mess up. • Be animated, cheerful, excited. • Be loud and clear. • Introduce yourself at beginning and thank the audience at end. • **Have fun!**	• Do not stop and restart if you make a mistake or forget. **Just keep going no matter what.** • **Do not apologize** for making a mistake or forgetting. • Do not be bland and monotone. • Do not fear. Your audience only wants you to succeed. • **You do not need to be perfect.**

4.8 SPEECH TIME

It's finally time to give your big speech. **Section 4.8.3** tells you exactly how to give your speech. Then, **Section 4.8.4** provides information for scoring and analysis of this lesson. Before we get to that though, it's time to prepare your audience and yourself.

First, **we strongly recommend that you videotape all of your speeches, especially this Introductory Speech, for future reference (and for fun).**

When you're ready, set up the camera or phone and assign someone to take the video. We recommend that you capture the top two thirds or more of your body and keep background distractions to a minimum.

4.8.1 AUDIENCE PREPARATION

Your audience has no interactive role in this lesson. When it is time, **you or someone you assign** should bring the audience into your "auditorium" and seat them in the proper place for your speech. **The audience should be given instructions** similar to the following once they are seated:

> BE SURE TO DO AN INTRODUCTION, OR ASSIGN AN "ANNOUNCER" TO INTRODUCE YOU!

- *"Welcome and thank you for attending - Student's Name - speech. Your participation is critical to the success of the Gabberz speech training program.*

- *- Student's Name - will be out shortly and give a 2 to 3 minute speech on "Famous Speeches of History."*

- *Please hold your questions until after the speech. Your comments afterward will be greatly appreciated.*

- *We would like input on the Speaker's delivery of the speech such as confidence, volume, stance, eye contact, connection with the audience, smiling, etc.*

- *Please keep the comments short, constructive, and related to the delivery of the speech, NOT the content.*

- *Immediately after the comments, - Student's Name - will present the speech again to make adjustments to the original delivery.*

- *After the second speech, you will receive an assessment sheet to rate the speaker. You may work together to provide a single composite score. Please be honest, but fair.*

- *Now, Ladies and Gentlemen, it is time. With a round of applause, I'd like you all to welcome - Student's Name - ."*

You don't have to do it exactly this way, use your imagination or embellish if you like. For multiple students, do the introductions for each other. Just remember to try and make this an "event" for everyone.

4.8.2 STUDENT PREPARATION

By now, everything should be ready and you should be prepared for your first speech.

- You have practiced out loud at least 10 times.

- You have your speech in hand.

- Your audience is seated and has received instructions.

- The video camera is running.

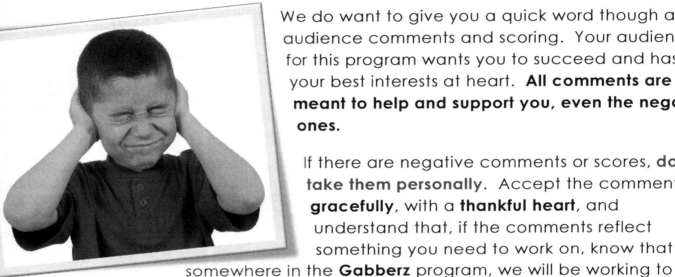

We do want to give you a quick word though about audience comments and scoring. Your audience for this program wants you to succeed and has your best interests at heart. **All comments are meant to help and support you, even the negative ones.**

If there are negative comments or scores, **do not take them personally.** Accept the comments **gracefully**, with a **thankful heart**, and understand that, if the comments reflect something you need to work on, know that somewhere in the **Gabberz** program, we will be working to improve that skill. **Remember, you do NOT have to be perfect!**

And now... it's speech time !

4.8.3 INTRODUCTORY SPEECH

This is a simple reading speech and all instructions are provided within the speech itself. Keep the following points in mind when you get up to give your speech.

- When you are introduced step in front of your audience, **smile** at them, and begin in a loud, **clear voice**.

- You can refer to the written speech as much as you need to. **You don't need to memorize it**.

- Make an effort to entertain your audience with a fun speech. Don't speak in a monotone, **use your voice as a tool** to move and motivate your audience.

- Follow the instructions and **try to have fun with it.** Your audience will not judge or make fun of you. **They want to have fun WITH you.**

- Your audience has made the effort to support you and attend your speech. Although you do not have to be perfect, **give them your best effort!**

- Go forth. Speak clearly. **Be a proud Gabberz!**

4.8.4 ANALYSIS & SCORING

So, now that you've given your first speech, we have to ask you a question? Did the things you were worried about happen? If any of it did, was it as bad as you thought?

We bet it wasn't. In fact, we'd bet you even had a little fun. Guess what? It gets even more fun.

So, how'd you do? **Were you perfect? Of course not. You're not expected to be.** The reason we do the analysis and scoring on all the lessons is to help you learn your strengths and weaknesses. That way, you can work to improve and build upon your strengths over time.

So, what is scored? We'll use the goals we set in the beginning of the chapter and a couple of other speech guidelines to look at specific accomplishments. Each lesson will have its own analysis and scoring.

Who scores the speech? Get your audience to provide feedback and then do a self-assessment and score yourself. You could even choose to have speeches professionally analyzed by **Gabberz Coaches.**

How does the scoring work? At the end of each lesson, there's an *Analysis & Scoring* page. The page will have instructions as to who fills it out and the things to be scored. If your audience is providing input, you will either give them your book with the page in it, or you can copy the page and give it to them. All members of your audience will work together to come up with a single score in each category. You will fill out your own assessment after they are done.

The next page is your **Analysis and Scoring Sheet** for the Introductory Speech. **Hand the sheet to your audience as soon as you have completed your speech event.**

ANALYSIS & SCORING SHEET – INTRODUCTORY SPEECH

AUDIENCE SCORING SHEET:

Audience Members: please work together to come up with one score for the speaker in the identified categories. Please provide honest input to help the speaker identify strong skills and areas for improvement.

AUDIENCE, Please rank the following categories from 1 to 5 where: 1 = Needs Work/Strongly Disagree 3 = Average/Agree 5 = Excellent/Strongly Agree	1 to 5
The Speaker accomplished the goal of this lesson by giving a speech of 2 to 3 minutes duration <u>twice</u>.	
The Speaker appeared prepared and did more than just read the speech.	
The Speaker talked clearly and loud enough for the audience to hear.	
Although the Speaker was allowed to read from a prepared speech, the Speaker looked at or engaged with the audience to some degree.	
The Speaker smiled during the speech.	
The Speaker varied voice and tone to make the speech interesting.	
Comments:	

SELF-ASSESSMENT BY THE STUDENT:

Please rank yourself fairly to see how you improve over time.

STUDENT: Rank the categories from 1 to 5 where: 1 = Needs Work/Strongly Disagree 3 = Average/Agree 5 = Excellent/Strongly Agree	1 to 5
I did not die or receive grievous bodily injury.	
I was not embarrassed giving the speeches.	
I was not nervous giving the speeches.	
The speech was easier to give than I thought it would be.	
The speech was easier to give the second time.	
I felt prepared and ready when the time came.	
I had fun and enjoyed giving the speeches.	
I was comfortable looking the audience members in the eyes and interacting with them.	
I understood the directions and instructions for this lesson and had no problem completing the task.	
I learned that this is not hard to do.	
I learned that this is fun.	
Comments:	

4.9 CONGRATULATIONS! PREPARE FOR LESSON 1

Congratulations on doing the Introductory Speech. We know you did great and are well on your way to becoming a *Gabberz Master Speaker™*. Here's what to do next.

- **FIRST!** Thank everyone for their support and let them know that you have another speech in about **2 weeks**.

- **Take a deep breath and relax.** But not too much, there's work to be done for Lesson 1 in the next chapter.

- You'll again be reading a prepared speech. You'll also have to do some writing. Don't worry; we'll help you build your speech. We'll even give you the topic.

> TRY TO GET EVERYONE TO SCHEDULE NOW WHILE THEY'RE STILL IN THE ROOM.

www.gabberz.com

Public Speaking for Kids, Tweens, and Teens
Level 1, Single-Student, Do-it-Yourself

CHAPTER 5

LESSON 1 — KNOW FEAR = NO FEAR

What You'll Learn in This Chapter:

✓ Use emotion and passion to create more impact.

✓ Avoid creating your own anxiety and minimize fears.

✓ List your concerns and overcome them.

5 LESSON 1—KNOW FEAR = NO FEAR

5.1 OVERVIEW

5.1.1 INTRODUCTION

Have no fear, Gabberz is here! Although there is nothing to fear from speaking in front of others, some people do feel terrible anxiety or nervousness even thinking about it. You might even be feeling anxiety now as you prepare for this speech. That's fairly common and perfectly fine.

SUGGESTION !
On this first lesson, we suggest you read <u>all</u> of Chapter 5 first before you do any of the lesson, then go back to Section 5.2.2. This will help you get the hang of it.

The **good news is that there is nothing to fear** and we're going to show you how to use any anxiety or nervousness that you might be feeling to make your speech even stronger. So prepare for a fun ride and let's get started. Here's the **Overview Table**:

Lesson 1 Overview	
Preparation Time	2 Weeks
Schedule	Date _____ Day _____ Time _____
Lesson	You will read one prepared speech <u>and</u> prepare a 2nd speech through an exercise. Both speeches will be 2 to 3 minutes long.
The Exercise	You'll create a worksheet comparing the good and bad things about giving speeches. Then, you'll give a speech based on the worksheet.
The Speech	You'll read the Gabberz-provided speech in **Appendix B. DO NOT read this speech yet!** Wait until your speech event—We'll tell you what to do when the time comes.
Goals	You will learn that, even if you are nervous or anxious, there is nothing to fear in public speaking AND that you can use your anxiety-driven emotion and passion to add greater impact to your words.

5.1.2 ALL ABOUT FEAR AND EMOTION

5.1.2.1 GENERAL

We'll be working on two speaking areas during this lesson: **fear** and **emotion**. These are closely tied together and we'll learn to use them to improve your skills, generate excitement, and find joy in speaking.

Really put your heart into this lesson and give it your best.

5.1.2.2 FEAR

Okay... maybe we should fear <u>this</u> guy.

Franklin D. Roosevelt said, "**There is nothing to fear but fear itself.**" Possibly... but if there *are* things in life that deserve a healthy fear, speaking in front of others is **not** one of them.

For our purposes, when we talk about fear, we are talking in general about the different concerns that might worry a speaker:

- stage fright,

- performance anxiety,

- nervousness,

- being judged,

- making mistakes,

- being wrong,

- boring people, or

- a fear of being the center of attention (or social anxiety).

Even if you did feel any of these things, the first thing to understand is that **these are "internally focused" things that your audience generally will not see or notice**. And even if they do, so what?

None of these things will cause you physical harm or any kind of mental damage. And most

Public Speaking for Kids, Tweens, and Teens – Confidence for Life!

Gabberz

are not important to your success. Okay... if you continually **bore people**, they might not want to hear you speak any more. But we'll show you ways to easily overcome that problem.

Unfortunately, many people who have even the slightest fear of speaking in front of others will find ways to avoid any situation that involves speaking. You are **not** going to go down the avoidance path. You're going to **embrace any fears or nervousness** you might have and use it.

Remember — **your audience wants you to succeed**.

Our problem as speakers is that we often read too much into what **we think** our audience is thinking, *not* what they **actually** are thinking. Consider the following:

- **"Oh no, the audience is staring at me blank-faced while I'm speaking."** You might think they are bored, totally uninterested, or you are being judged. The opposite may be true. Many people generally listen in a passive way. Blank faces can be listening faces.

- **"The audience is looking at my sweaty hands."** They are not. They don't know your hands are sweaty, they don't care, and they will never notice unless you call attention to it.

The audience does not know what's going on in your mind and they generally cannot see things you might feel such as nervousness, anxiety, or sweaty hands.

Most importantly, **your audience does *not* know what you were _going_ to say, they only know what you _actually do_ say**.

A little nervousness or anxiety is **normal** and, in fact, might help inject some energy into your speech. Here are a few tips to help you out in the beginning and then we'll move on.

- **Ignore most advice:** Over time, you will receive much advice on how to eliminate your fears. These might include staring off above your audience's heads; memorizing every word; and even envisioning your audience in their underwear. Don't be lured into

these tricks to bypass the issue. Your fears will eventually just fade. In the meantime, you want to learn to **embrace and use** them to energize your speeches.

- <u>**Focus on your audience**</u>: Concentrate on your audience, **not** on your internal dialogue or feelings. Think about how the audience will enjoy your presentation, rather than your nervousness. Ignore your sweaty hands. Focus on the positive response of your audience, NOT on your internal fears.

- **Speak <u>with</u> your audience, don't perform <u>at</u> them:** You don't need to be perfect, you simply want to **connect with your audience and communicate** your message to them.

- **Do not try to "read" your audience:** Until you have experience "reading" an audience correctly, just assume they are happy and enjoying your speech. If *you* place other feelings on them, you're focusing on yourself, not on your audience.

- **Concentrate on <u>one person</u> at a time:** Some people prefer to look at the audience as a large, single mass and talk to **it** in general— as if the entire audience is just a single person. That puts distance between you and your audience and makes it hard to connect. **You <u>may</u> find it easier to focus on one person at a time.** After all, your audience sees you as one person they are having a conversation with. Try pretending like you're having a series of conversations with individuals. **Just be sure to change your focus often** or you'll make someone very uncomfortable.

  "Eye've" got my "I" on you !

  - **Be grateful:** With your concentration on the audience rather than yourself, you can focus on the positive. Be grateful that the audience is there, grateful that they trust you to speak in front of them, grateful that they are all healthy and safe. **Fill your mind with positive thoughts** about the audience, not negative thoughts about your performance.

    - **Visualize:** Visualization (picturing yourself in a certain situation doing a certain thing correctly) has proven to be extremely effective in almost all activities. The best athletes always visualize themselves making the shot or winning, and speakers must do the same. Do you think you will do better by thinking about how

nervous, anxious, or fearful you're going to be? **Or** by visualizing yourself giving a successful speech that everyone loved? Picture yourself in the room where you're going to give the speech. Picture your audience being receptive, smiling, and applauding. **Picture yourself as confident, self-assured, and capable.**

One last thought on fear. Do you remember the first time you finally got the nerve to ride that **really insane roller coaster**? Do you remember the feeling in your gut as you stood in line to board? How about as the car rattled to the top of that 10 story climb, and you waited for the coaster to slip over the edge? **That nervous energy was exhilarating... terrifying and exhilarating.** As you went over the crest and dove toward the ground, you were pumped full of energy and excitement... and fear! **That's what you want to use during your speeches.** If you're nervous, anxious, tingly, even terrified, **use that pent-up energy to energize your speech**. The ride will be terrific.

5.1.2.3 EMOTION

Fear is an emotion. You'll use many emotions to strengthen your message. Right now, you'll concentrate on **passion**—a positive emotion to counteract the *potentially* negative emotions generated by fear.

Everyone knows passion. Maybe you're passionate about skateboarding; maybe it's music, or dance, or karate, or football. **If you convey your passion** for something when speaking to others, **it adds tremendous impact** to the information you're sharing.

People generally want to believe what you are telling them. A flat monotone voice, without variation or movement, gives the impression that you don't care or are not convinced the information is true or important. **If you don't care, why should your audience**?

However, **if you feel passionate about something and let the passion come through when you're speaking, it has a great emotional impact on your listener.** They don't have to agree with you, but there'll be no denying that you care about the issue/topic being discussed.

Your passion poured out into your words will make your speech not only believable, but also entertaining, enjoyable, and memorable.

Here are a few tips on using emotion.

- Try to **pick topics you have some passion for.** That's not always possible, especially if someone else chooses the topic for you. If you have to give a speech on a topic you don't have passion for, at least try to be animated and vary your voice. Never give a speech in a flat, dull monotone... no matter how boring.

- Never fake your emotions. You can enhance, embellish, or exaggerate **a little**, but never try to fake it except for **obvious** humor. You will come across as fake and possibly even a liar.

- **You will of course ignore that advice while doing Gabberz** because there are times when **we're going to have you exaggerate – a lot!**

- People naturally try use all of their senses to gather information and form opinions. They (mostly subconsciously) process the tone of your voice, your perceived emotions, your body language, etc. All of this counts so **it's important that your emotion matches the content and importance of your words.**

- Help your audience feel what you're feeling and your speech will become much more memorable.

5.1.3 GOALS

There are two main goals of this lesson. If you don't get it all now, that's okay! It will all come together for you in later lessons.

1. **Goal 1**: Learn to **identify any fears, anxieties, or other concerns you have** about speaking in front of others. If you don't have any, great! Many people don't. If you do have fears, anxieties, or concerns, that's great too! You'll learn to use those to your advantage to add energy and passion to your speech. Relax and have fun with this.

2. **Goal 2**: Your goal here is to **learn the impact passion has** on your words and your audience. You'll exaggerate (quite a bit actually) to understand that you can combine words, feelings, actions, and a little drama to **incorporate all the senses** of your audience.

5.2 PREPARE

5.2.1 WHAT YOU'LL BE DOING IN LESSON 1

We'll start out with our regular "**What You'll Be Doing**" table.

What You'll Be Doing – LESSON 1	
What	You will be doing an exercise (and writing your own speech from that) **AND** reading a Gabberz prepared speech.
When	Date _____ Day _____ Time _____ Give yourself about **2 weeks** to do this lesson.
Who	Try to schedule your speech with **as many people as possible**. You will not need anyone to assist you.
Where	Your audience will not be interacting with you on this speech (except to laugh, cry, and applaud) so they can sit anywhere.
Prepare	Some preparation will be required for the exercise portion. **VERY IMPORTANT**: This lesson is **NOT** about giving a great speech. This is about getting up, pushing your comfort levels a little bit, and just doing it.
EXERCISE — Lesson 1	
What?	You'll create a worksheet describing the worst you can imagine happening during your speech on one side, and the best you can imagine on the other. Then you'll create a speech based on your list. **Section 5.2.2** provides details.
Length?	**2 to 3 minute speech** read at normal speaking speed. Time yourself during practice.
SPEECH — Lesson 1	
What?	You'll also be reading the Gabberz-provided speech **in Appendix B**. <u>**DO NOT**</u> look at or read the speech until directed to do so during your speech event.
Length?	2 to 3 minute speech read at normal speaking speed.
Special Notes	No preparation is required for this speech as you will not see the speech until you are ready to give it. Now, here's our twist... you must follow the directions in the speech to give it with **highly exaggerated emotions**. The emotions will change. It will be challenging and lots of fun!
Subject?	You'll find out when you read the speech.

START EARLY, YOU'LL NEED TIME TO PREPARE!

Public Speaking for Kids, Tweens, and Teens – Confidence for Life!

5.2.2   EXERCISE—WHAT'S THE WORST THAT COULD HAPPEN?

Come back here **after** reading chapter.

Seriously, what's the worst that could happen?
We want you to **reach way down deep** and write down your worst possible fears, **the most terrible things you could imagine happening** or going wrong. Really stretch and **get it all out in the open right now.**

Booo! I'm a Fear Monster.

Don't hide your fears for later. Don't let a nagging concern fester and rot in the back of your brain. **Let's deal with it now so you can put the fear monsters behind you.**

You'll write down all the negative things you fear or are concerned about when you speak in front of other people. Then you'll list all the positive things you feel. You'll put these side-by-side on a sheet of paper, compare them, and then you'll write a passionate speech about the results.

Let's get started!

1. Grab a sheet of blank paper and a pen.

2. Draw a single line down the middle of the paper. Title the left half, *"What's the **Worst** That Could Happen?"* Title the right half, *"What's the **Best** That Could Happen?"*

3.   On the left side, start a list of the kinds of **things you fear might happen.** List anything you're concerned about. These could (but don't need to) include: *I might make mistakes; I might forget my speech; people might laugh at me; I might be criticized;* etc. **List everything that's on your mind.** It's important.

4. **See the example** we've provided on the next page.

5. Leave some space to the right of each of these things you fear or are concerned about.

6. Now, go back to each of those things you listed and write down **how it would make you feel if it happened.** For example, if you wrote down, *"I'm afraid I'll forget part of my speech,"* **then write down next to it how you think that would make you feel.** Maybe something like, *"It would make me feel stupid."*

What's the WORST that could happen?

- I could make a mistake. — I would be embarrassed.

- xxx

- xxx

- xxx

- xxx

- xxx

- xxx

What's the BEST that could happen?

- I will be confident. — I'll be happy.

- xxx

- xxx

- xxx

- xxx

- xxx

- xxx

7. You don't have to do this all at once. Take your time and try to capture it as it occurs to you. When you're done with the left side, we'll move on to the right.

8. On the right side of the paper you're going to do the same thing for the positive things. You're going to **list the good things that you want to happen.** These could include things like: *I will do a great job; I will be confident; the audience will like my speech; I will remember all the important parts*; etc. Remember to leave some space to the right of this list.

9. Now, go back to each of the good things you've listed and write down how it would make you feel if that happened. For example, if you wrote down, "*the audience will like my speech,*" **then write down next to it how that would make you feel if it happened.** Maybe something like, "*I would feel proud of my work.*"

10. Take your time and try to capture everything. **Visualize yourself giving the speech and think of all the positive events and outcomes.** You'll want to have this worksheet complete before you take the next step.

Hopefully, you've captured your worst fears and concerns so you can put them to work for you. Two important points here.

- **First**, notice we did not say you were going to banish your monsters. Instead you're going to **harness them** to help you.

- Second, you have to realize that in most cases, **your worst fears will not happen**.

It's okay to feel these fears and anxieties. It's perfectly normal. What it means though is that **you can't let any of that stop you or hold you back**. By identifying and exploring these monsters, you can make them your friends and get them to work for you.

You're going to start this process by **writing a speech from the worksheet** you just developed.

And, because we don't like boring, we're throwing in a fun little twist for you. The speech you give **MUST be given with highly exaggerated emotion** throughout. If it's something that you fear — *cringe, act fearful, maybe even let out a little scream*. If it's something that might make you sad — be *very, very sad* (maybe add some fake crying).

You must keep up this emotional onslaught for the entire speech. No matter how you tie it together, no matter what is between your points, you must do it all with highly exaggerated emotional delivery.

Use your body, use your voice, use your eyes, hand gestures, whatever it takes. Even fall to your knees if you have to. **You want your audience to <u>feel</u> your emotion**. It should be easy, especially for the stuff on the left side of the sheet. If it's something you fear enough to write down, you should be able to express that fear—loudly. If it's something that makes you feel good, you should be able to express your passion.

Over act! Be bold! Be outrageous!

Let's get started on your exercise speech!

Before we move on to the **Gabberz-provided** speech in **Appendix B** you're going to give, we wanted to give you a few more tips on putting together and writing this exercise speech.

> *Start writing your speech **EARLY**. You want plenty of time to practice before your speech event!*

- You're speech should be **2 to 3 minutes long** (you should shoot for 3 minutes). That's about 250 to 400 words at normal speaking speed.

- However, considering the emotion you're putting into this, you may have pauses, repetitions, and other things that eat up time. You may want to write part of the speech and time that to see how you're doing before finishing. If you run over, that's okay.

- **There's <u>no wrong way</u> to structure this speech.** You could approach it many ways. You could do all the sad stuff, then all the fear stuff, then all the happy stuff. Or, you could mix dread, then happy, then fear, then proud, jumping from one emotion to the next. Or, you could tie each negative to a positive that counteracts it (**see the following graphic** with arrows showing what we mean). **You can do it any way you want.** Look at your list and see what feels good to you. Then go for it!

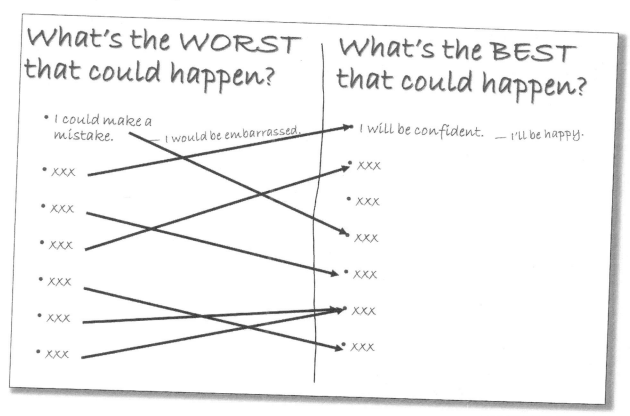

- **There's also <u>no wrong way</u> to write the text you're going to use**. You could use your introductory speech to talk about how you felt these things before, but not after. You could talk about how you dealt with them before this speech. You could talk about how you're going to overcome your fears and concerns. **Or, you could just expand on each good and bad item on your list and just go hog wild with it, getting outrageous, pouring on the emotion.**

- Your speech **doesn't have to make any sense**. It **doesn't** have to tell any tale. **It can be as nonsensical as you can imagine.**

> **IMPORTANT! THE MORE YOU OVER-ACT, THE MORE FUN YOU AND YOUR AUDIENCE WILL HAVE.**

- Write whatever you need to that will help you spill out emotion and hammer your audience with your passion. **You really need to let go and act, act, act!**

By the way, **we highly recommend that you keep all worksheets and speeches you write in a safe place** in case you want to see or refer to them later. You may even be asked in a future lesson to come back to some of these earlier speeches.

Let's move on to the second half of your event—the Sealed Speech.

5.2.3 SPEECH—EMOTION SPEECH

Preparation for the sealed speech is a little easier. Well, to be truthful, it's a lot easier. **We've written it for you** (the speech is located in Appendix B). **DON'T GO THERE YET—this is a sealed speech!**

You cannot prepare. **You should not peek until it is time for you to give the speech in front of your audience.** You'll then open it and read it live to your audience—following the instructions that are included in it.

Here's the fun part. You must also give this speech with greatly exaggerated emotions. The speech will include instructions for where to express emotion and what emotion to use. You need to quickly read the directions to yourself, then act on them as you read the text that follows.

Here are a few tips:

- Use your preparation for the exercise speech to help you let loose with emotions on this one. You don't know what you'll have to do, but **you'll know what you are capable of.**

- You'll do the sealed reading first, before the exercise speech so you can use this as a warm-up to get your full emotions geared up and ready to rock.

- The <u>first page</u> of **Appendix B** is an instruction sheet to you. You can read that page now, but **don't** go any further!

- The emotional directions in the speech will be clearly visible. Continue that emotion until directed to do another emotion.

- It's okay to pause a few moments when you get a new direction so you can gather yourself and go for it. However, **try to be quick** so you don't lose the momentum.

You must **really let yourself go and pour out the *inner ham* that's inside you.** Now is <u>not</u> the time to be shy. After all, **you are only doing what *we* told you to do.** All blame can be laid on Gabberz. **You, however, can claim all glory.**

5.3   PRACTICE (FOR 2 SPEECHES)

PRACTICE FOR YOUR APPENDIX B SPEECH.
No practice is necessary for the speech. The emotions you practice in your exercise will help prepare you, so be sure to **work on a wide range of emotions** in your exercise speech so you'll be ready for anything.

PRACTICE FOR YOUR EXERCISE SPEECH.
By now you should have completed the speech you wrote from your exercise paper. It's important that you concentrate on getting your speech written early so that you have time to edit, modify, and practice. **Don't wait until the last minute—it will show.**

- Always practice out loud, preferably at the volume you intend to use during your live event.

- You should practice the first couple of times without the exaggerated emotion so you can get a good feel for the speech and how it flows. Or doesn't. **Remember, there's no wrong way to write this speech, it can be as free-flowing, random, or chaotic as you like.** It does NOT have to be good literature.

- After you've got a feel for the speech, start adding emotion. Get as outrageous as you can. You want to overshoot the mark here.

- As we've done up to this point, **it's not necessary or required for you to memorize the speech.** You may rely on a printout of your text, or notes, or cards, or whatever you are comfortable with.

- If you have time, continue practicing while you concentrate on expanding and embellishing your emotions. Feel free to add more as you go along. Add movements, gestures, etc. to make the experience enjoyable and memorable for your audience.

- **Your emotions and actions are WAY more important in this lesson than the actual words** you speak. Don't worry about getting it just right or forgetting parts. Just keep going and have fun with it.

- Whenever you practice, **visualize** yourself in your "auditorium" giving the speech to your actual audience. Imagine yourself being successful, confident, and strong. If you can really see yourself that way, you will be.

- **There's no wrong way to do this one** as long as you get up, do the speeches, and apply some emotion to them.

5.4 PRESENT

It's almost time for your Lesson 1 speech event. Here are a few final notes before the big show.

1. Remember to verify that everyone still plans to attend.

2. If you have prepared any props, tools, or anything else that you'll use during the speech, verify that they are ready and work as you anticipate. Do a dry run or two if possible (set everything up and practice as if it were the actual event, just don't let anyone see).

3. The day of the event, double-check to make sure you have everything you need, such as a copy of both speeches.

Finally, review the **Do/Do Not Table** on the next page for a quick list of the things you'll want to do vs. the things you should avoid.

Public Speaking for Kids, Tweens, and Teens – Confidence for Life!

DO/DO NOT TABLE
Lesson 1

DO	DO NOT
• Exaggerate everything! • Use your body, your hands, your feet, your eyes, and your voice to "convince" your audience that you are truly feeling these emotions. • Keep going, even if you mess up. • Be super animated to keep the energy and momentum up. • Concentrate on your audience, not yourself. • Be loud and clear. • Introduce yourself at the beginning and thank the audience at end. • Have fun!	• Do not stop and restart if you make a mistake or forget. **Just keep going no matter what.** • **Do not apologize** for making a mistake or forgetting. • Do not be bland and monotone. • Do not concentrate on what's in your mind, **concentrate on the audience.** • Do not throw up. • You do **not** need to be perfect, or correct, or even close.

5.5 SPEECH TIME

Most all lessons will be structured this way:

1. Audience Preparation

2. Student Preparation

3. Speech/Exercise Details

4. Analysis & Scoring

Professional Video Analysis

Don't forget, Gabberz can provide you a **detailed professional analysis and feedback** of your speech videos.

Visit www.Gabberz.com for more information.

Don't forget to video your speech event so you can see how it all came together.

5.5.1 AUDIENCE PREPARATION

The audience does not have a role in this speech except to sit back, enjoy it, and provide you input afterwards.

When it is time for your speech event, you or someone you assign should bring the audience into your "auditorium" and seat them in the proper place for your speech. **The audience should be given instructions similar to the script on the following page** once they are seated (either by you or by your assigned Announcer).

- "Welcome and thank you for attending *- Student's Name -* speech for Lesson 1.

- *- Student's Name -* will be out shortly and give two speeches of 2 to 3 minutes each.

- We have a very interesting and exciting event for you today. For the first speech, *- Student's Name -* will be opening and reading a speech the student has never seen before.

- The speech will include instructions that the student must follow live. We'll find out what's going to happen together.

- Immediately following that speech, *- Student's Name -* will present a prepared speech based on the fears and anxieties of giving speeches. That ought to be fun!

- After the second speech, you will be given a scoring sheet for a consensus score. Please provide honest feedback.

- Now, Ladies and Gentlemen, it is time. With a round of applause, I'd like you all to welcome *- Student's Name -* ."

Use your imagination or embellish or change the introduction however you like. You can do it yourself or ask someone in your audience to help you. **Make it exciting!**

5.5.2 STUDENT PREPARATION

You should be ready and prepared for the speeches. There's not much else but to get out there and do it. Make sure everything's ready.

- ✓ The audience is seated and has been told what to expect.

- ✓ You have your speeches and this book in hand.

- ✓ Someone has been assigned to start the video camera. It can be on a tripod (preferable) someone can hold it.

- ✓ You have the audience score sheet in this book handy so the audience can enter their scores and comments.

Remember to **accept all suggestions and advice gracefully and gratefully.** Everyone wants to help you. Remember, you are not trying to be perfect here; you're only trying to reach the goals we set.

And now... it's speech time!

5.5.3   LESSON 1 SPEECH AND EXERCISE

Here's generally how the event should run. **It's okay if it doesn't work out just this way,** or if you want to change it. **Do whatever works for you.**

Gabberz Prepared Speech:

1. After the introduction, step up in front of your audience to the designated spot (make sure it's the right spot for the camera). Carry only the Gabberz-prepared speech in **Appendix B** (either this book or a copy).

2. Smile at the audience and greet them in a confident, clear voice with the following...

3. Hold up the **speech** and say something like, "*Ladies and Gentlemen, I have never seen this speech, let's see what happens together.*"

4. Take a few moments to gather yourself.

5. Begin reading and really **give it your best.** Put as much emotion as possible into the speech.

6. When done, thank the audience to let them know you're done. When the applause dies down, let them know the second speech will start in a few moments.

Exercise Speech: THE EXERCISE SPEECH, STEP-BY-STEP!

7. Step off-stage for a few moments to catch your breath. Grab whatever notes or papers you need for the Exercise Speech.

8. Have the Announcer provide you another **short** introduction.

9. Step in front of the audience, give them a big smile, and begin the second speech in a **loud clear voice**.

Remember, you can use these wide outside margins to take notes!

10. Refer to your speech/notes as much as you need to. You should know it well, but **you're not required to memorize this one**.

11. **Pour emotion into your delivery.** You should be warmed-up from the first prepared speech and be much more comfortable throwing the emotions out there now. Just give it your best.

12. When you're done, **thank your audience**. Then get them to fill in the scoring sheet while everything is fresh in their minds.

Your audience has made the effort to support you and attend your speech so, although you do not have to be perfect, **always give them your best effort!**

The purpose of Gabberz is as a training program for you, but you want to make an effort to keep your audience's interest as much as possible so they'll keep coming back again and again for all of your speeches. **Keep it fun and be proud of what you're doing!**

5.6 ANALYSIS & SCORING

This is the second speech you've done now. Any permanent scars? Any war wounds? Did the things you put on the left side of your sheet happen as you'd thought? How about the right?

We'd bet things went just fine. We'll even venture to say you and your audience had a fun time.

More importantly, no matter how it went, you saw that any fears or concerns you might have had **did not stop you from doing this**. You saw that you can get up in front of people to give a speech... maybe you can even act out a little and be a little silly. What is the worst that could happen?

Even if you "messed up", even if you forgot parts, even if you had trouble doing the emotions you'd planned on, **so what?**

You got up and did it, therefore, you were successful. Congratulations!

The next page is your **Audience Analysis and Scoring Sheet** for this lesson. **Hand this book or a copy of the sheet to your audience as soon as you have completed your speech event.**

Your personal **Self-Assessment Checklist** follows this scoring sheet. You should complete that yourself as soon as the event is over. Try to be honest with yourself.

ANALYSIS & SCORING SHEETS – LESSON 1

AUDIENCE SCORING SHEET:

Audience Members: please work together to score the speaker appropriately. It is important to provide honest input to help the speaker identify strong skills and areas that need work.

AUDIENCE, Please rank the following categories from 1 to 5 where: 1 = Needs Work/Strongly Disagree 5 = Excellent/Strongly Agree	1 to 5
The Speaker gave 2 speeches of 2 to 3 minutes each.	
While reading the **Sealed Speech** in the envelope, the Speaker made an attempt to convey strong emotions.	
While giving the **second speech**, the Speaker made efforts to convey very strong emotions throughout the speech.	
The Speaker was engaging and kept our interest.	
The Speaker did **not** appear nervous or anxious.	
The Speaker talked clearly and loud enough for the audience to hear.	
The Speaker smiled at the audience appropriately.	
The Speaker varied voice and tone to make the speech interesting.	
Comments:	

SELF-ASSESSMENT BY THE STUDENT:

STUDENT: Rank the following categories from 1 to 5 where: 1 = Needs Work/Strongly Disagree 5 = Excellent/Strongly Agree	1 to 5
I got up and did the speeches and survived without permanent damage to body or limb.	
The worksheet helped me identify any fears or concerns I had and reduced my worry about them.	
None of the bad things I worried about happened.	
The good things I hoped for did happen.	
I had fun and enjoyed giving the speeches.	
I was able to express the emotions I had intended to.	
I believe the audience enjoyed the speeches.	
I learned that when I use emotion along with the words, I feel better about the speech.	
I can use my nervous energy to energize myself and my words.	
I understood the directions and instructions for this lesson and had no problem completing the task.	
Comments:	

5.7 CONGRATULATIONS! PREPARE FOR LESSON 2

Congratulations on completing your first full lesson. We're sure you did a great job and you're even more excited than before.

Here are a few things you need to do to prepare for Lesson 2.

- **FIRST!** Thank the audience for their support and let them know that you have another speech in about **2 weeks**.

- **We suggest that you read ALL of Lesson 2 before starting any of the work on it.** There's one speech and a great exercise with it.

www.gabberz.com

Public Speaking for Kids, Tweens, and Teens
Level 1, Single-Student, Do-it-Yourself

CHAPTER 6

LESSON 2—THE 3 PS

What You'll Learn in This Chapter:

✓ How to **P**repare properly.

✓ How to **P**ractice effectively.

✓ How to **P**resent successfully.

6   LESSON 2—THE 3 P'S

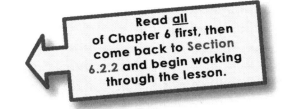
Read **all** of Chapter 6 first, then come back to Section 6.2.2 and begin working through the lesson.

6.1   OVERVIEW

6.1.1   INTRODUCTION

The success of a speech relies a lot on prior proper preparation and practice. We're going to concentrate a little bit this time on proper techniques for **Preparation** and **Practice** to get to an exciting **Presentation** (the **3 P**'s).

We're going to spend a little less time talking about things and more getting you actually doing this lesson. Here's the Overview Table:

Lesson 2 Overview	
Preparation Time	**2 Weeks**
Schedule	Date _____ Day _____ Time _____
Lesson	You will **prepare one speech this time** and you'll need to write it. Don't worry; we'll help you with the process.
Exercise	You will do a **short warm-up vocal exercise** to build rapport (a connection) with your audience.
Speech	Your speech will be an action story that you write. It can be something that actually happened or something totally made up. You will need to **move and be animated**.
Goals	Gain experience writing a speech and preparing for its delivery.

6.1.2   HOW TO PREPARE AND PRACTICE FOR YOUR SPEECH

6.1.2.1   GENERAL

Practice is considered a part of preparation and proper preparation is critical to the success of your speech. Don't skimp on preparation. **You deserve more and your audience deserves more**.

Proper preparation:

- improves your delivery;

- reduces nervousness;

- combats any fears or concerns you have;

- focuses your topic; and

- improves your audience's experience.

If you are not prepared, your audience will notice and you don't want to start out with a negative. Do everything you can to **make this a positive experience for everyone**. Here are a few short tips.

1. **Start Early**: We've mentioned this one before. Start as soon as you have an assignment. If you wait, it will get much harder. **START EARLY, ACT QUICKLY, AND BE DECISIVE!**

2. **Know Your Audience**: Before you do anything, make sure you know what type of audience you'll have, the occasion, where you're going to speak, and how much time you have.

3. **Choose Your Topic Quickly**: Don't waste valuable time trying to come up with *just the right* topic for your speech. This is a real time killer where nothing happens. **Make a decision and go for it.**

4. **Schedule Your Time Goals**: You have your topic and the date of your speech. Get out a calendar and look at the number of days you have to write and practice. That time is going to go quickly. **Set goals** to make everything happen on time.

5. **Have Conversations**: When you decide on a topic, it may be helpful to have conversations with family or friends about your subject. You may get some great ideas or identify some things that people want to know about that are related to your topic.

6.1.2.2 SOME SPECIFIC WRITING TIPS

We worked on coming up with topics for your speeches in an earlier lesson. Hopefully, you got some ideas and have them written down. We'll give you the topic for this one, but first, here are a few tips on actually writing a speech.

1. **Don't Fret, Just Do It**: Making a quick decision on your topic is the most important thing you can do to get started. **You can always change your mind later** if needed, but you'll find that your first instincts are frequently correct.

2. **Outline it First**: Writing your speech will be much easier if you start by writing a simple outline. Grab a sheet of paper, put down an idea for your beginning at the top, an idea for closing at the bottom, then an idea for the body halfway between those two. Once you have those, it becomes simpler to fill in the blanks between them. Just follow the path from beginning to end, step-by-step.

3. **Write a Single Sentence**: Start out with a single-sentence. Something to catch your audience's attention and prepare them for what's to come. This is the **"theme"** of your speech and will help keep you focused as you continue writing. But it all starts with getting once sentence down on paper.

4. **Keep Research in Perspective**: If you are doing research to write your speech, be careful not to waste too much time over-researching. Get the research you need, then start writing your paper.

5. **Start with Simple Sentences, Not Paragraphs**: Start with simple sentences or brief sentence fragments for each major point (according to your outline). Don't try to write it all now. **Just get the important points down in the proper place**. Once you have these, the rest will start flowing naturally.

6. **This is NOT a Script**: Remember, you are not writing a script that you're generally going to memorize word-for-word. You'll identify the information you want to convey to the audience, learn that information very well, and then "talk" to them.

7. **Write Quickly and Recklessly**: Don't over-think your writing when you start. Just write quickly, capturing your first thoughts and getting them down on paper. **There'll be time later to edit, rewrite, and fix**. Your first draft will never be perfect. If you worry about making this first draft perfect, you'll struggle to ever finish.

8. **Short and to the Point**: Keep all of your sentences short and to the point. This will help you focus your meaning and remember each of your points.

6.1.2.3 SOME SPECIFIC PRACTICE TIPS

You know the old saying, "*Practice makes perfect.*" **Well... ignore that.** Remember, we **don't** want "perfect." Try this old saying (*that we just made up*) instead, "**Practice makes comfort.**" That's more like it! Here are a couple of practice tips for you.

1. **Power Opening**: Work hard on developing and practicing a powerful opening. If you give a powerful, **audience-grabbing opening** with an emotional hook, you draw your audience in immediately and you'll have them captivated for the rest.

2. **Power Closing**: Ditto on the closing. The final 5 to 20 seconds should be powerful, emotional, and personal. The power opening hooks them in; the power closing makes it memorable.

3. **Loud and Proud**: Always practice out loud at the volume and speed you intend to use during your live event. **Anything else is not practice.** If you feel you need to go off deep into the woods to practice your speech privately to the squirrels, please do so. They're known to enjoy a good speech from time-to-time.

4. **Stuffed Animals**: Speaking of squirrels, it helps to practice your speech in front of others. If you can't get people, you can use stuffed animals, action figures, pets, or even potatoes with faces drawn on them to act as your audience. This helps you learn to focus on the audience so you can practice eye contact.

   That's very captivating. Do you have any spare nuts?

5. **Hand's Free Speaking**: You'll eventually learn to memorize the information in your speeches. In the meantime, you can use short notes or cards to refer to. Don't memorize word-for-word, get comfortable with the content.

6. **Highlights**: Use as few words as possible for notes or cards. You should only need a reminder of the next point, not the text. Remember, you're *talking*, not *reciting*.

Public Speaking for Kids, Tweens, and Teens – Confidence for Life!

7. **Don't over Practice**: Get very familiar and comfortable with your material. **Learn the content well.** Don't memorize the speech and recite it word-for-word. **We rarely write the way we speak** and the speech will sound stilted, unnatural, and appear to be memorized. Find a balance that lets you be you: comfortable, charming, and brilliant as always.

6.1.3 GOALS

Remember, **we're still at the point where you cannot do these lessons wrong**, *as long as you do them.* Here are the two goals for Lesson 2.

1. **Goal 1**: The first goal is to work on how to write a speech, including developing a theme, outlining, key points, editing, and timing.

2. **Goal 2**: The second goal is gaining experience in *preparing* for a speech, including practicing, delivery, power openings, power closings, and audience interaction.

6.2 PREPARE

6.2.1 WHAT YOU'LL BE DOING IN LESSON 2

Here's your simple breakdown of what you'll be doing in Lesson 2.

What You'll Be Doing – LESSON 2	
What	You'll be doing a voice exercise with the audience, then giving a speech that you wrote.
When	Date _____ Day _____ Time _____
Who	Schedule **as many people as you are comfortable with.** The more you have in your audience, the more fun it will be.
Where	Your audience will be interacting with you during the exercise so they should be seated facing you.
EXERCISE — Lesson 2	
What?	See **Section 6.2.2.** You should have loads of fun with this one. All you will be doing is yelling random syllables at your audience (ba, la, ge, ig, anything you like). You will also instruct your audience to yell these back at you as quickly and loudly as they can (can you see where larger audiences will be more fun?).

Length?	You should do this for approximately 1 minute. Try to judge your audience's enjoyment of the exercise to determine if you should go shorter or longer. But never go too long, you always want to leave your audience wanting more.
SPEECH — Lesson 2	
What?	See **Section 6.2.3**. You'll need to write, practice, and give a speech. The more you get into this, the more fun it will be. You will write an "action" story. While telling it, you must be very animated, giving exaggerated hand movements and moving around the stage.
Length?	3 to 4 minute speech read at normal speaking speed.
Subject?	Your subject for this speech can be any kind of "action" story you like. **It can be true, exaggerated, or completely made up.** Just remember your requirements for animated movements throughout. So, it should be something with lots of action that you can mimic or show physically.

COME BACK HERE AFTER READING THE CHAPTER.

6.2.2 EXERCISE—YOU HAVE PERMISSION TO YELL!

Rarely is it appropriate or acceptable to yell at your family or, really, at anyone. In this case we'll make an exception (with a little warning). So, what's going to happen?

First, you will let your audience know that you are going to yell random syllables at them for one minute or so before your speech. You can yell any syllables you like such as **ah, bah, ge, be, ig**, etc. The stronger, and more forcefully you can yell them out the better. **This is <u>not</u> the time to be shy.**

The real fun though comes when you instruct your audience that they must yell those same syllables right back at you as quickly and loudly as they can. If you yell "**GA!**" at them, they need to immediately yell "**GA!**" right back at you. If you like, you can even ask them to stand up and do it.

You *could* say something like, "*Before I get to my speech, **those awful people at Gabberz** want me to yell at you. Mom, Dad, remember, you bought this program for me, so you can't get mad at me for doing what I'm supposed to do. Oh, they also want **you** to yell back at **me**. If I yell 'HAH!', you have to yell 'HAH!' right back at me as quickly and loudly as you can. Okay?*"

The more people you can get yelling at you, the more fun it will be.

There's not much preparation needed for this exercise. If you like, you can write down a bunch of syllables and sounds on a card for a prompt.

What's the point? Is it just to torture you? *Probably* not. There's (almost) always a reason behind our madness. Part of being comfortable speaking in front of others is just realizing that you <u>can</u> do this type of stuff and the world won't come to an end. Get comfortable doing things out of your "**comfort zone**" (things you're comfortable doing) often enough, and you **become comfortable with yourself.**

"So, when I smacked into the wall, I looked kinda' like this..."

6.2.3   SPEECH—ACTION SPEECH

It's time to get animated! No, we're not talking cartoon animation. We're talking about you being animated... moving, pointing, gesturing, mimicking, etc.

You'll need to put on your acting cap for this one. The end result will be a **3** to **4** minute speech with you acting out the action the entire time. That means a couple of things:

1.   You'll have to work harder at learning the story of your speech because you'll be moving and gesturing the entire time. Remember, you won't "memorize" your speech, you'll learn the "story" so that you can "tell" it to your audience.

2.   You'll have to write a little longer speech this time. This should be fairly easy though. You'll either be telling a story about something that actually happened to you, or you'll be making up some wild adventure just for fun.

Oh, and did we mention the other part of this speech? In addition to the movement and action you'll be doing, you also need to try and **make direct eye contact with each member of your audience** throughout the entire story.

Me thinks he hath gone nuts!

Challenging!

Let's get started writing your speech with some ideas:

1. This will be a **3 to 4 minute speech**.

2. Remember that speaking at normal speeds averages 120 to 175 words per minute. That means you'll need to write a speech of about **350 to 600 words** or so. That's not very hard at all if you're writing about something you're interested in.

3. Where to get ideas? They're all around you. Let's start with your Scribbling Book (or Notes). Maybe there's a good adventure story in there. Where have you been? What have you done? Has anything exciting, dangerous, or painful every happened to you?

4. If not, start thinking about where you've been and what you've done. What tales of adventure do you tell your friends when you get together?

5. Or maybe you just want to **make up a wild adventure**. Travels in space. Epic underwater battles. Fighting off fat Ninja Warriors who want the last slice of your birthday cake. Your imagination has no limits—and neither does this speech. Get wild.

You don't have to have the perfect idea. Just something interesting.

> **START EARLY AND DECIDE ON A TOPIC QUICKLY.**

1. **Write down your opening sentence**. Make it something exciting. A teaser. Something to make your audience perk up with interest. To use our example, maybe something like, *"Did you know I was nearly assassinated on my birthday fighting off overweight Ninjas?"* We guarantee that will get your audience listening.

2. **Now, write down your closing sentence at the bottom of your paper.** Something that wraps things up nicely and leaves your audience wanting more. Maybe something like, *"So, as the fat Ninjas stumbled away, I felt sorry for them and offered to share the cake. That's when the skinny Sumo Wrestlers showed up."* The end.

3. **Now, go to the middle of the paper.** Write down some short notes on the main action that happened between the opening and closing. You don't need all the detail or flow, just the primary points of action.

4. **Now, you can start filling in the white space.** What happened before the main action? Who are the fat Ninjas? Why are they after you? What happened after the main action? How did you ultimately defeat them? Be sure to include a lot of action during every moment of the speech. You'll need to be acting out the movements throughout your entire speech, so **be sure there's physical stuff going on**.

"When I did this... they got scared and ran away."

So would we, Johnny...
So would we.

Hopefully, you've now got an **exciting action story** loaded with plenty of opportunity for movement and over-acting. If all went well, you've also got a story that you'll be eager to share with your audience. **You'll see how much easier it is to remember and tell your story when you are excited and interested in it.** This excitement helps you remember and it engages the audience.

For this lesson, the words are not as important as the physical action used to draw your audience in.

6.3 PRACTICE

Practice for the Yelling Exercise

There's not much to do to practice for this. You could write down a list of sounds to yell, then practice yelling them to get used to it.

Practice for the Action Speech

You will definitely want to practice this speech since it will be hard for you to refer to your written notes while you're giving it. You'll have a tough time finding your place while you're jumping around, acting out the action, while also maintaining eye contact with the audience.

1. **Start writing your speech early.** Don't wait until it's perfect to start practicing (you're not reading it word-for-word anyway). As soon as you have a first draft, begin practicing.

2. **Always practice out loud.** And in this case, **practice the movements and actions** you're going to perform.

3. **Make big colorful notes on your speech.** It might help if you get a fat red marker and write down some cues, notes, and directions.

4. **Learn your story.** You are NOT memorizing the speech word-for-word. You are learning your "story" so you can "tell" it. **Just as if you were telling the story around a campfire.**

6.4 PRESENT

It's almost time. Here are a few final notes before the big show.

1. Remind everyone that your speech is coming up.

2. Do a dry run or two if possible before the event.

3. Before you bring everyone into your "auditorium", make sure you have everything you need so they are not waiting on you.

Finally, review the **Do/Do Not Table** for a quick list of the things you'll want to do vs. the things you should avoid. Don't worry if you do some do not's or do not do some do's. Eventually it will all be second nature to you.

DO/DO NOT TABLE Lesson 2	
DO	**DO NOT**
• **Smile** at your audience. • Stand tall and straight. • **Keep the action going** throughout the entire speech. Make your audience "feel" your story. • Try to keep **eye contact** with everyone in your audience during the entire speech. Focus on them one at a time, moving from person to person. • **Keep going**, even if you mess up. • Be animated, cheerful, excited. • Be **loud** and **clear**. • Introduce yourself at beginning and thank the audience at end. • Have fun!	• Do not stand like a statue. **Keep moving.** Use the whole room if you need to. • Do not stop and restart if you make a mistake or forget something. **Just keep going no matter what.** • **Do not apologize** for making a mistake or forgetting. • Do not be bland and monotone. • You do not need to be perfect. • Try not to break any furniture while acting out your story.

6.5   SPEECH TIME

Remember, there are four pieces to the "Speech Time" section:

1. Audience Preparation
2. Student Preparation
3. Speech/Exercise Details
4. Analysis & Scoring

Those four sections are where you'll find all the details of exactly what you need to do and how to go about it. Oh, and don't forget to record your speech event to video—you'll be glad you did.

6.5.1   AUDIENCE PREPARATION

The audience will have a roll during the **Yelling Exercise**, but not during the **Action Speech**. You should let them know this up front.

When it is time for your speech event bring the audience into your "auditorium" and seat them in the proper place. **The audience should be given instructions** similar to the following once they are seated.

- *"Welcome and thank you for attending* - **Student's Name** - *speech for Lesson 2. Your participation is greatly appreciated."*

- *There are 2 parts to today's event. We need your help on the first.*

- *The Speaker will yell random nonsense syllables at you and you all need to yell them back as* **quickly and loudly as you can**.

- *Don't be shy, put your hearts into it and do your best to out-shout the student.*

- *The second part is an action speech. The audience does not have a role except to sit back and enjoy the story.*

- *At the end of today's speech, you will be asked to complete a short survey about today's event.*

- *"Now, Ladies and Gentlemen, it's time for the exercise and speech. With a round of applause, I'd like you to welcome* - **Student's Name** - *."*

Public Speaking for Kids, Tweens, and Teens – Confidence for Life!

6.5.2 STUDENT PREPARATION

Everything should be ready and you should be prepared for the event.

- You have practiced out loud **more than 10 times**.

- You know your "story".

- Your audience is seated.

- They've been given instructions.

    - The video camera is running. We leave it up to you whether to record the introduction or not. You can always record the introductions and then trim them out later.

THE EXERCISE, STEP-BY-STEP!

And now... it's time for your Event !

6.5.3 LESSON 2 EXERCISE AND SPEECH

You'll be doing the exercise first, and then you'll be doing the speech you prepared.

6.5.3.1 EXERCISE

1. As soon as you're introduced, step up in front of your audience (make sure it's the right spot for the camera).

2. Smile at your audience and thank the "Announcer" for the kind introduction and thank them for their applause.

3. Give them a quick reminder of what you'll be doing (yelling random syllables which they must yell back as **quickly and loudly** as they can). Remember the introductory statement we gave you back in **Section 6.2.2** about those "*awful people at Gabberz*"? Now would be the time to use that if you like.

4. Once they agree, pause for a moment, take a deep breath, then **let them have it with both lungs!**

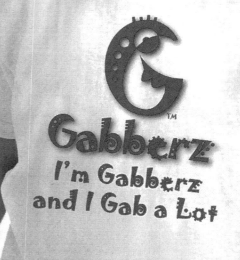

5. Just **keep going**, without pause.

6. The tricky part is "**reading**" your audience. You need to be able to tell when they're still having fun and stop before they get tired of it. You want to **leave them wanting more**.

7. When you think they've had enough (but no more than about a minute and a half), stop, take a deep breath, and **thank the audience for their help** so they know you're done.

8. A **fun twist** (optional) would be to start walking off stage, then suddenly turn and give them one more big, loud yell for them to return. But only do that once.

THE SPEECH, STEP-BY-STEP!

6.5.3.2 SPEECH

1. As soon as you step off stage, your designated "Announcer" should step up and say a few words by way of introducing you for the speech portion. He might thank you, thank the audience, then say, "**Ladies and Gentlemen, a round of applause for our next speaker, ____Student's Name____.**"

2. As soon as you're introduced, step up to your spot again.

3. Take a deep breath, smile at your audience, and then launch into your speech.

4. Start right out with **lots of action**, **movement**, and **physical demonstration** of your story.

5. Try to maintain some eye contact with the people in your audience. Change your focus from person to person; making sure each of them gets equal attention.

6. Make an effort to entertain your audience with a fun speech. Get excited, **use your actions as a tool** to move and motivate your audience.

7. **Try to have fun with it**. Your audience will not judge you or make fun of you. **They want to have fun WITH you**.

8. Your audience has made the effort to support you and attend your speech. Although you will not be perfect, **give them your best effort!**

Go forth. Speak clearly. **Be a proud Gabberz!**

6.6 ANALYSIS & SCORING

Congratulations, you have another lesson under your belt. We're not very deep into this, but you should be starting to see how this is working for you. You should also be having a **whole bunch of fun**. It only gets more exciting as we go along.

We really hope you poured some emotion and passion into this lesson. That's how you'll get the most out of it. But, as we've been saying all along, **you cannot do any lesson in Level 1 wrong**. As long as you get up and do it, you are successful and it will help move you along to becoming a *Gabberz Master Speaker*.

You know what else? Anytime you feel like it, you can go back and re-do a speech. If you'd like to try it again, just ask your family to gather sometime and do it. They will be supportive of your dedication.

So, **what did you learn this time**? You learned that you can get up and interact with your audience for fun. You learned that you can move around and that this **movement keeps your audience's attention** on your story. And, you learned that you can write an interesting speech.

That's a lot for one lesson!

By now, you should also be feeling just a tiny bit of that **wind in your face**. Nothing bad happened. You had a good time. Your audience had a good time. It's time to start thinking about taking off the training wheels and really getting into it.

The next page is your **Analysis and Scoring Sheet** for this lesson. Hand the sheet to your audience as soon as you have completed your speech event.

Your **Self-Assessment Checklist** follows that. You should complete that yourself as soon as the event is over while everything is still fresh in your mind. Try to be honest with yourself.

ANALYSIS & SCORING SHEETS – LESSON 2

INSTRUCTIONS FOR AUDIENCE SCORING:

Audience Members: please work together to score the speaker in the identified categories. Please provide honest input to help the speaker identify both strong and weak skills.

AUDIENCE: Please rank the following categories from 1 to 5 where: 1 = Needs Work/Strongly Disagree 3 = Average/Agree 5 = Excellent/Strongly Agree	1 to 5
The Speaker and/or the Announcer gave clear instructions to the audience on what was going to happen.	
The Student completed an exercise where the Speaker yelled random syllables at the audience (who responded).	
The Speaker was loud and engaging during the exercise, and appeared to be having fun.	
The Speaker then told an "action" story describing some event or activity.	
During the speech, the Speaker was animated, moving around to demonstrate the action in the story.	
The Speaker tried to maintain eye contact with the audience.	
The Speaker appeared to "know" the story and told it with emotion and passion.	
The Speaker appeared prepared and did more than just read a speech to the audience.	
Comments:	

Public Speaking for Kids, Tweens, and Teens – Confidence for Life!

SELF-ASSESSMENT BY THE STUDENT:

Please rank yourself fairly so you can see how you improve over time.

STUDENT: Rank the following categories from 1 to 5 where: 1 = Needs Work/Strongly Disagree 5 = Excellent/Strongly Agree	1 to 5
The audience did not "boo" me or tar and feather me and run me out of town on a rail.	
I was not embarrassed doing the exercise or the speech.	
I had fun and enjoyed doing the exercise and giving the speech.	
I felt prepared and ready when the time came.	
I was comfortable maintaining eye contact with the audience.	
I think the audience was much more engaged in my story because I was moving around, acting out the action.	
I found it was pretty easy to write the speech using the tips provided in this and earlier chapters.	
I understood the directions and instructions for this lesson.	
I learned that this is not hard to do.	
I had more fun this time than in the previous lessons.	
Comments:	

6.7 CONGRATULATIONS! PREPARE FOR LESSON 3

Congratulations on completing this lesson. You learned a lot and you're well on your way to becoming a *Gabberz Master Speaker*.

Here are a few things you need to do to prepare for Lesson 3.

- **FIRST!** Thank everyone for their support and let them know that you have another speech in about **2 weeks**.

- When that's done, **take a deep breath and relax**.

- You'll need to do some preparation for Lesson 3, so get started early. The speech will be a little different format this time.

www.gabberz.com

Gabberz Public Speaking for Kids, Tweens, and Teens
Level 1, Single-Student, Do-it-Yourself

CHAPTER 7

LESSON 3—YOU'LL PUT YOUR EYE OUT!

What You'll Learn in This Chapter:

✓ How to comfortably make eye contact with your audience.

✓ How to form and present questions to your audience.

✓ "How to 'Read' your audience.

Public Speaking for Kids, Tweens, and Teens – Confidence for Life!

7 LESSON 3—YOU'LL PUT YOUR EYE OUT!

7.1 OVERVIEW

7.1.1 INTRODUCTION

SUGGESTION! Read *all* of Chapter 7 first, then start working at Section 7.2.2.

Speaking to others is about **communication**, not putting on a show. You must connect with your audience and try to create some type of emotional relationship between you and them.

One of the most effective ways to accomplish this is through eye contact—the simple act of looking someone in the eye when you're talking to them. This will be a continuing theme throughout the program, but Lesson 3 will get you started.

Lesson 3 Overview	
Preparation Time	**2 Weeks**
Schedule	Date _____ Day _____ Time _____
Lesson	You do not have to write or read a speech. You will need to come up with some questions for your audience.
Exercise	You will practice staring at your audience and learn to "read" their reactions.
Speech	You will come up with a series of questions and you will concentrate on making eye contact while interacting.
Goals	You will learn how to be comfortable making eye contact and how to read your audience's reaction.

7.1.2 MAKING EYE CONTACT IS NATURAL

7.1.2.1 GENERAL

Have you ever had a conversation with someone who never looked you in the eyes while they were talking to you? How did you feel? What did you think? When someone doesn't look at the person they're talking to, most people have one or more of the following reactions.

- They don't trust the person speaking.

- They don't believe the person speaking.

- They don't think the person speaking is interested in them.

- They don't think the speaker knows what they're talking about or are unprepared.

- They find it harder to "like" someone who is not making an effort to connect with them.

Obviously, these are **not** things you want people to think about you when you're speaking—either to an individual or to a group. You want to be trusted and believed.

Do you trust me?

The solution is simple. Learn to connect by making proper eye contact.

7.1.2.2 THE WRONG WAY

There are a lot of "**old school**" techniques that have been taught to speech students to help them **hide their discomfort** with making eye contact.

As with many "old school" teachings, we don't like that. **Masking or hiding a problem doesn't resolve it. The real solution is to fix a problem, overcome it, or <u>use it</u> to your advantage**. That's a process we're going to start in this lesson. That's assuming you even have a problem with eye contact to begin with. Many people don't.

Here are some of the <u>**wrong ways**</u> that have been taught to "pretend" you're making eye contact with your audience.

- "*See your audience as a big blur, not as individuals?*" **Wrong!** That just masks the problem and prevents a connection.

- "*Look at a person's forehead or mouth instead of their eyes?*" **Nope!** People can see right through that one.

- "*Scan the back wall of the room or look at different objects that are near people, but not at the people?*" **Yikes!** You might as well just talk to an empty room.

- "*Think of the audience as one person with many heads?*" **Not even close!** Similar to seeing the audience as a blur, it only masks the issue and prevents you from connecting with them.

You see, it's <u>not</u> just about the audience connecting with you; **it's also about *you* connecting with your audience.** If you're just **hiding** behind a mask, YOU are not connecting. When you connect with your audience, you will be more engaged, animated, excited, and effective.

There's no shortage of advice you'll hear about how to mask or hide from problems. Don't get pulled into that trap.

Does that help?

7.1.2.3 THE RIGHT WAY

There *are* actually many ways to get there, but **the end result must be that you become comfortable making eye contact with anyone you're having a conversation with.** If it's an individual, that person must feel that you are interested in them, the topic, and you are engaged in the discussion. If speaking to a group, the individuals in the audience must feel you are, at least in part, talking directly to them.

So, how do you go about making eye contact natural and effective? Here are a few tips and we'll continue to work on this in later lessons where you'll learn more.

No, we didn't think so.

- **Practice, practice, practice.** Just like public speaking in general, making eye contact becomes easier the more you do it. Push yourself to make sure you do it in all conversations and soon you'll find that it is natural and comfortable for you.

- **Look for positive people.** You never know what people are really thinking, but you can make some assumptions and use that to your advantage. Start out by looking for the most positive, engaged people who are smiling and nodding as you speak. Look at them first to gain encouragement, then engage with those who don't "appear" as positive. Remember what we said earlier; many people who sit stone-faced, without expression, are actually enjoying the speech. You just can't tell at the time. Even if you have someone who doesn't like your speech, it is important that you give everyone their fair attention.

- **Think outwardly, not inwardly.** As you look people in the eyes, your inner thoughts should be along the lines of, "What you can I do to give them a better experience," **not**, "I'll just die if they don't like my speech."

• **"Read" your audience.** While you are making eye contact, you can get a better idea of how your audience is reacting to you. Some may smile; others may nod, cock their head, look down, look away, frown, shake their heads, or do nothing. You'll learn to quickly read what your audience is silently saying to you so that you can adjust your speech, pace, or intensity to give them the best experience.

7.1.3 GOALS

We have three main goals for this lesson. Most importantly... relax, have fun, and **let that inner ham out** every time.

1. **Goal 1:** The first goal is to gain just a little bit of confidence in making eye contact with your audience.

2. **Goal 2:** The second goal is to learn to "read" your audience.

3. **Goal 3:** The third goal is to gain experience interacting with your audience by asking them questions.

7.2 PREPARE

7.2.1 WHAT YOU'LL BE DOING

Now it's time to learn what you'll be doing in Lesson 3.

What You'll Be Doing – LESSON 3	
What	You'll be doing an audience exercise (**Section 7.2.2**), then asking them a series of questions you will prepare (**Section 7.2.3**).
When	Date _____ Day _____ Time _____
Who	Try to schedule your speech with **as many people as possible**. It's not a requirement, but it will be more exciting and fun.
Where	This lesson is highly interactive with your audience so you should do this in a location where you can interact with each other.
Prepare	Very little preparation is required for the Exercise. The speech is actually a series of questions you'll need to ask your audience. You'll need to come up with a topic and write those.

EXERCISE — Lesson 3	
What?	This is a warm-up exercise to provide you an easy introduction to eye contact. It should be fun for you and your audience.
Length?	1 to 2 minutes depending on the size of your audience.
SPEECH — Lesson 3	
What?	You will pick a topic (something you know, or something entirely made up) and write a series of rapid-fire questions to ask your audience. You must make strong eye contact when asking.
Length?	2 to 3 minutes of questioning. You will generally not allow your audience to fully answer the question so timing will be important.
Subject?	Student may choose the topic.

COME BACK HERE AFTER YOU'VE READ THE ENTIRE CHAPTER.

7.2.2 EXERCISE—AN EYE FOR AN EYE

Once again, we're going to reach deep into the arena of what might be slightly outside of your comfort zone. If you really get into it, this should be a lot of fun for you AND for your audience. To help them get into it, you're going to prepare them for what about to happen.

When you're ready to begin, you might say something like, "*Can you believe it, now **those awful, <u>mean</u> people at Gabberz** want me to stare at you. First it was yelling, now it's staring. Oh, they also want **you** to stare back at **me** and **try to distract me** or **make me laugh** to break my concentration.*"

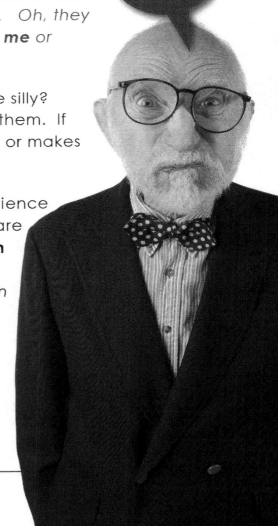

Do you have someone in your audience that is a little silly? Maybe a little sister or little brother? You'll start with them. If possible, you want someone who either laughs easily or makes you laugh easily.

Begin the exercise by picking **one** person in your audience and focusing your attention on them. Feel free to stare stone-faced or motionless. **Just put your full attention on them for 15 seconds or so**. If the person starts to smile or appears to be on the verge of laughing, *then* you can step in closer and exaggerate. Try and get them to break up just by staring.

You should also try and **maintain your calm**. They may try to make you laugh, or distract you; you should only let this happen if it will cause them to laugh also.

After about **15 seconds** (it doesn't have to be anywhere near exact, just whatever feels "right"), move on to someone else. Again, try to pick out someone who is on the verge of laughing or cracking up.

You should be sure to give nearly equal attention to everyone in your audience. Don't leave anyone out.

Most importantly, you need to **"read" your audience to see how long you should keep this up**. This exercise should be 1 to 2 minutes. If everyone looks uncomfortable, bored, unsure what to do, you should keep it short and move on to the speech portion.

You **don't** have to apologize, just smile and say, *"That's it, my goal this lesson was just to look you in the eyes."* If everyone's having fun, laughing, trying to make you laugh... you should run it a little longer.

Remember; always leave your audience wanting more!

7.2.3 SPEECH

This one's not so much a speech as it is fast-paced interaction with your audience. You'll need to prepare some material and know it well to pull this off. When you do, it'll be a lot of fun!

This "speech" consists entirely of you asking questions of your audience. We'll talk about how to prepare you questions in a moment. First, here's what you'll need to do for this speech:

1. You must ask your questions of the audience quickly... one after the other.

2. You must go to a different audience member for each question.

3. While questioning the audience member, you must make full eye contact with them the entire time.

4. These can be real OR nonsense questions like, "**Quick, if a butterfly is flying north, how does it taste?**" (Answer: *With its mouth, silly.*)

5. You **may** give them up to 5 seconds to answer. <u>OR</u>, you might choose not to give them any time at all and move rapid-fire around the room, drilling each person with questions that you *don't give them time to respond to*. This is *your* choice.

7.2.3.1 WRITE YOUR QUESTIONS

You'll want to keep this questioning up for **2 to 4 minutes**. Depending on how long you give your audience to respond, you'll need probably 25 to 50 questions.

What will your questions be about? All you need is a topic and come up with a bunch of related questions. **Remember, the questions <u>don't</u> have to make sense and they don't have to be able to be answered**.

- You can ask questions about something you know a lot about. That makes it easy for you to come up with questions.

- You can ask questions *you* know nothing about. Maybe it's a topic your audience knows about.

- Grab your nearby Encyclopedia and pick pages at random.

- Pick a topic and just ask random questions that generally no one would know the answer to. For example: let's say you pick "Politics". Your rapid-fire questions could be:

  - How many nickels would it take to pay for the national debt?

  - If you stacked those nickels, how high would they reach?

  - What government agency would be in charge of stacking those nickels?

  - What sound would it make when they fell over?

You see? Even though our topic was politics, the questions strayed way off topic. It usually works better if they stream with a common theme like above, but go anywhere you like.

And when your audience tries to answer the questions rapid-fire, you can snap back, "*Yes! Correct!*" or "*No! Wrong answer!*" (Even if the answer was correct.) Then move on quickly.

Just remember that **you** are in charge of the questioning and responsible for keeping the momentum and the fun going. Oh, and don't forget about maintaining **eye contact**.

7.3 PRACTICE

7.3.1 PRACTICE FOR YOUR EYE CONTACT EXERCISE

There's not much you can do to practice for this one unless you want to stare at your dog or your stuffed Teddy. You really just have to prepare mentally and **commit to doing the exercise no matter what happens**. Just try to have fun with it.

7.3.2 PRACTICE FOR YOUR QUESTION SESSION

This one will be a little tougher. You'll need to maintain your stream of thought while concentrating on maintaining eye contact and reading your audience.

You can use written questions, or note cards, or whatever you like to keep you on track, but any tool will be hard to use while **keeping up a fast pace** during this question session.

The best advice we can give you is to write your questions well, study them, practice them, and **get to know your material**. The most exciting way to pull of this "speech" is to know your material well enough that you can go around the audience, firing off your questions as a "**stream of consciousness**". All that means is that as you ask one question, the topic, words, or answer from that logically lead you to the next question without having to think about it.

Think back to our "nickel" example earlier. We started out with one question about nickels (*How many nickels would it take to pay for the national debt?*). Now that we had a topic about nickels, we would have 30 or 40 things we could ask. If we'd studied and knew our questions well, they should just pop into our heads as we grilled the audience.

If you're not comfortable with that, you could write down a cue word or <u>short</u> phrase on 3x5 index cards and have a stack of those handy to quickly pull from. Be VERY careful of two things if you use this method.

1. **Don't write down the whole question.** If you're reading the question to your audience, it's pretty hard to maintain eye contact with them. Use just a word or two.

2. **Pull the cards fast, but DON'T DROP THEM.** (Although you *could* consider tossing them dramatically over your shoulder right after you ask each one. **Just don't put anyone's eye out;** that's the **wrong** way to make **eye contact**.)

7.4 PRESENT

Here are a few final notes before the big show.

1. Remind all of your audience members of the date and time.

2. If you have prepared any props, tools, note cards, or anything else that you'll use during the speech, verify that they are ready and work as you anticipate. Do a dry run or two if possible (set everything up and practice as if it were the actual event).

3. The day of the event, double-check to make sure you have everything you need, such as whatever tool you'll be using to help cue you for your questions.

4. Try to **assign someone** to do your introductions.

Finally, review the **Do/Do Not Table** for a quick list of the things you'll want to do vs. the things you should avoid. Don't worry if you **do** some **do not's** or **do not** do some **do's**. Eventually it will all be second nature to you.

DO/DO NOT TABLE Lesson 3	
DO	**DO NOT**
• Smile and engage with your audience. • Look your audience in the eye and talk directly to them. • **Only speak when are looking your audience in the eye.** • Use lots of vocal variety to keep your audience interested. • Make your transition from one person to the next natural and comfortable. • Be fast, loud, and clear.	• DO NOT speak while **reading** your notes or text. Read your cue quickly, then look and speak. • Do not stop and restart if you make a mistake or forget. **Just keep going no matter what.** • Do not be hesitant—just plunge ahead fearlessly. • You do not need to be perfect.

7.5 SPEECH TIME

As always, **we highly recommend that you videotape your exercise and speech**. You might want to get someone in your audience to hold the camera and capture you as you move around.

7.5.1 AUDIENCE PREPARATION

Your audience has a role in both the exercise and the "speech". In the exercise, they will be trying to break your concentration. In the question portion of your speech, your audience will be trying to answer your questions. It's up to you if you give them time to answer or not.

Bring the audience into your "auditorium" and seat them in the proper place for your speech. The audience should be given instructions similar to the following once they are seated.

YOU OR YOUR ANNOUNCER NEED TO DO AN INTRODUCTION.

• *"Welcome and thank you for attending* - **Student's Name** - *speech for Lesson 3. Your full participation is critical to the Student's success in the **Gabberz Public Speaking Program**."*

• *"There are two events today. The first is a short exercise, and the second is a question and answer session."*

• *"During the first exercise,* - **Student's Name** - *must practice making eye contact with the audience. You are encouraged to try and distract or fluster the student."*

- "During the speech portion, instead of a speech, *- Student's Name -* will be required to rapidly ask the audience a series of questions, while maintaining eye contact with the person being questioned."

- "You must try to answer the questions as quickly as you can, keeping the momentum going."

- "You probably won't have a correct answer. Any answer—right or wrong—will do. Just answer fast! Assuming *- Student's Name -* allows you the time to answer at all."

- When the session is done, you will be asked to fill out a short survey rating the student's efforts today."

- "Now, Ladies and Gentlemen, it is time. With a round of applause, I'd like you to welcome *- Student's Name* ."

Use your imagination or embellish the introduction if you like. If there are multiple students, do the introductions for each other. If there is only one student and a small audience, you can do the introduction yourself (with appropriate adjustments). Try and make this an "event" for everyone.

7.5.2 STUDENT PREPARATION

By now, everything should be ready and you should be prepared for your first speech.

- You know your topic well and can ask the questions rapid-fire.

- You have notes in hand if you are going to use them.

- Your audience is seated.

- They've been given instructions.

- The video camera is running (someone will need to hold the camera since you will be moving around throughout the exercise and speech).

At the end of this, your audience may not be sure how to rate this event, it is quite unusual. Whatever feedback they provide, accept it gracefully and gratefully, taking it with the good will intended.

And now... it's speech time !

7.5.3 LESSON 3 EXERCISE/SPEECH

THE EXERCISE, STEP-BY-STEP!

You're ready, so it's time to go. The following list is "generally" how your event should go. If things happen differently, **that's okay**.

Exercise – Eye Contact

1. As soon as you're introduced, step in front of your audience, look them in the eyes, and smile.

2. This is where you might want to give that little introductory paragraph we provided to you previously. You know...

   *"Can you believe it, now **those awful, mean people at Gabberz** want me to stare at you? First it was yelling, now it's staring.   Oh, they also want **you** to stare back at **me** and try to distract me or make me laugh to break my concentration."*

3. You don't <u>have</u> to say this, you could say anything. Or nothing!

4. Now, take a deep breath, and say, *"Let's begin."*

5. Follow the instructions from **Section 7.2.2** to complete the exercise.

6. When you think the timing is right to stop, step back, and let the audience know this portion is done. You might say something like, *"See, that wasn't so bad after all."*

7. Thank your audience for their participation, then let them know the next session of the event will start in a few moments.

8. Step off stage for a few moments, grab your notes if you need them, and instruct your Announcer to reintroduce you.

THE SPEECH, STEP-BY-STEP!

Speech – Question and Answer

9. Step back out onto "stage" and give the audience a nice smile.

10. Take a deep breath, clear your throat, whatever you need to do, then pick your first target.

11. Make eye contact and fire off your first question.

12. From there, proceed quickly and deliberately.

13. Ask your questions **rapid-fire**, moving from person-to-person.

14. Keep the **momentum** going by keeping everyone engaged and participating.

15. Remember to **maintain eye contact** as much as possible.

16. **When you think the time is right**, end your session and thank your audience so they know you're done. It doesn't matter if you have not asked all of your questions. It's not about the answers.

17. Hand your audience the scoring sheet and ask them to complete that while this is fresh in their minds.

Although you are not "performing", make an effort to entertain your audience and keep them engaged.

Your audience made the effort to support you and attend your speech. Although you do not have to be perfect, **give them your best effort**!

Go forth. Speak clearly. Be a proud Gabberz!

7.6 ANALYSIS & SCORING

Wow, you have three lessons under your belt already. There's a way to go still, but you've got a lot of the basic material in your skill set now. You should be able to start using that in your other speeches as you move forward.

Were you able to comfortably maintain eye contact with your audience? Did it make you uncomfortable? Did it make your audience uncomfortable? If it did, that's okay. Comfort and skill come with time and practice.

Most importantly, once again, you got up and did it.

The next page is your **Analysis and Scoring Sheet** for this lesson. **Hand the sheet to your audience as soon as you're done.**

Your **Self-Assessment Checklist** follows that. You should complete that yourself as soon as the event is over while it is still fresh in your mind. Try to be honest with yourself.

Public Speaking for Kids, Tweens, and Teens – Confidence for Life!

ANALYSIS & SCORING SHEETS – LESSON 3

INSTRUCTIONS FOR AUDIENCE SCORING:

Audience Members: please work together to score the speaker in the identified categories. Please provide honest input to help the speaker identify both strong and weak skills.

AUDIENCE: Rank the following categories from 1 to 5 where: 1 = Needs Work/Strongly Disagree 3 = Average/Agree 5 = Excellent/Strongly Agree	1 to 5
The Speaker completed an <u>exercise</u> where he/she maintained eye contact with the audience at all times.	
The Speaker completed a <u>speech</u> event where he/she asked the audience a series of numerous questions.	
The Speaker asked the questions rapidly and gave equal attention to all audience members.	
The Speaker maintained eye contact with the audience members whenever he was speaking.	
The Speaker smiled during the exercise and question and answer session.	
The Speaker spoke clearly and maintained a comfortable volume level throughout the event.	
Comments:	

SELF-ASSESSMENT BY THE STUDENT:

STUDENT: Rank the following categories from 1 to 5 where: 1 = Needs Work/Strongly Disagree 5 = Excellent/Strongly Agree	1 to 5
I did not go blind looking into the eyes of my audience.	
I was not embarrassed during the eye exercise.	
I was not nervous during the question and answer session.	
I felt prepared and ready when the time came.	
I was comfortable looking the audience members in the eyes and interacting with them.	
I was comfortable asking my audience questions.	
I was able to "read" the audience and knew if it would be good to keep going or when to stop.	
I had fun and enjoyed giving the speeches.	
I understood the directions and instructions for this lesson and had no problem completing the tasks.	
Comments:	

7.7 CONGRATULATIONS! PREPARE FOR LESSON 4

Congratulations on completing this lesson. We hope you had fun!

Here are a few things you need to do to prepare for Lesson 4.

- **Take a deep breath and relax.** But not too much, there's work to be done for **Lesson 4**.

- Have you ever noticed the little crutches and fillers many people use in their speaking to fill voids? You know, "**ummm**," "**like**," "**ah**," and "**you know**" for example. Well, in the next lesson, we're like, you know, going to, ummm, work on eliminating those, uh, crutches and fillers.

www.gabberz.com

Gabberz Public Speaking for Kids, Tweens, and Teens
Level 1, Single-Student, Do-it-Yourself

CHAPTER 8

LESSON 4—UMMM CRUNCHER #1

What You'll Learn in This Chapter:

✓ How to identify verbal crutches.

✓ How to stop using verbal crutches while speaking.

✓ How to embrace silence without filling it with, "Ummm," "Ahhh," or "Like."

8   Lesson 4—Ummm Cruncher #1

Suggestion !
We suggest you read <u>all</u> of Chapter 8, then go back to Section 8.2.2 and begin working from there.

8.1   Overview

8.1.1   Introduction

You've heard them all before: **"ummm," "ahhh," "uhhh," "like," "you know,"** etc.

*Do I **look** like a verbal tic to you?*

These little **verbal fillers, tic's, or crutches** can quickly detract from an otherwise outstanding speech you are giving. They can also distract in day-to-day conversation so that the person you're speaking to becomes fixated on your **verbal tic**, and not your point.

This lesson will **begin** the process of limiting these **verbal fillers** from your speeches and from your conversations altogether.

Lesson 4 Overview	
Preparation Time	**2 Weeks**
Schedule	Date _____ Day _____ Time _____
Lesson	You will lead a short exercise, and then give a speech you have written.
Exercise	The exercise is a contest to see who can say these crutch sounds the longest without running out of breath.
Speech	You will write a speech on any topic you like and you must give it using as few verbal crutches as possible.
Goals	You will learn to recognize verbal crutches and reduce your reliance on them.

8.1.2   Time to Crunch the Ummm's

"Well, like, you know... it's time to like, get into the lesson and, you know, start doing, well... start doing it, like."

Hopefully, that's an exaggeration you'll never hear in real life. But verbal pauses are very common in our language and are there subconsciously for many reasons. Some of these include:

- to give ourselves time to **think or remember** the next point;

- to indicate to the listener that **more is coming**;

- to **hold our place** so that others don't interrupt us;

- out of **plain old habit** (we've become addicted to it);

- maybe just because we're **nervous**; or

- one of the biggest reasons—**we are uncomfortable with silence**.

There's a lot of debate about whether these crutches should be eliminated entirely or if a few here and there are okay.

Either way, **excess use** of any of these will distract your audience and cause them to be **thinking**, "*Gee, isn't it weird how that speaker uses 'like' in front of every sentence,*" <u>instead</u> of listening to your message. **Anytime you distract your audience** (either by a verbal tic, repetitive hand movements, or rustling papers) you risk losing their interest.

> I'm the "Ummm" Buster!

8.1.3 GOALS

We have two goals for this lesson:

1. <u>**Goal 1**</u>: **Reduce** your reliance on verbal crutches.

2. <u>**Goal 2**</u>: Stress **clarity** of thought and **concentration** on the activity at hand.

8.2 PREPARE

8.2.1 WHAT YOU'LL BE DOING

As usual, here's our little "What You'll Be Doing" table to give you an overview of this lesson.

What You'll Be Doing – LESSON 4	
What	You'll be doing an exercise with your audience (see **Section 8.5.3.1**), and then you'll give a speech you prepared (see **Section 8.5.3.2**).
When	Date _____ Day _____ Time _____
Who	Try to schedule your speech with **as many people as possible**. As always, the more people you can get, the more fun it will be.
Where	Your audience will be interacting with you on this speech so they should be seated fairly close to you with direct eye contact. They should be seated facing you while you stand. About TV distance should be good.

Prepare	In addition to writing and practicing your speech, you'll want to **start listening to yourself and others to try and identify all the little speaking crutches people use in everyday speech.**
EXERCISE — Lesson 3	
What?	This is a simple exercise based on a little game you'll play with your audience. You will provide them with a verbal filler such as, "**Ummm**," then instruct them to take a deep breath and on the count of 3 to say the filler as long as they can. The last one "**ummm'ing**" is the winner.
Length?	As long as you and your audience are having fun. Usually 3 to 5 fillers for one round is enough.
SPEECH — Lesson 3	
What?	You'll write a speech for this one. The topic can be anything, but we highly recommend that you **write it about something you're very familiar with** because you'll have to give this one without your speech or notes in hand. **Don't worry, you know you can do it!**
Length?	3 to 4 minute speech given at normal speaking speed. Time yourself during practice.
Special Notes	1. You cannot use your written speech or notes to give the speech. **You must learn it well enough to "talk" to your audience** about it. 2. You must try to avoid any verbal crutches. 3. Your audience will count usage of any of the crutches. 4. **If they count more than 20 uses of a filler**, you must give the speech a second time (but no more).
Subject?	This is an open topic speech. You can write about any topic you like so get out your **Scribbling Book** or notes and start thumbing through that. You should have a good list of topics to pick from. If not, start making a list of things you like to do, eat, see, play with, or study. Write about something exciting that you know well.

8.2.2 EXERCISE

Verbal crutches have become habit for many people and we don't really notice them until they're used in excess. At that point, they become annoying and distracting.

COME BACK HERE AFTER YOU'VE READ THE ENTIRE CHAPTER.

To **get your audience focused on identifying these crutches**, you will first provide them with a list of typical crutches, and then you'll lead them in a competition to see who can say them the longest.

There's not a lot you can do to prepare other than make a list of crutches to give your audience and pick some to compete with (probably "**um**", "**ah**", "**uh**", and/or "**so**").

I'm a champion ummmm'er.

Here's a list of the most common verbal crutches; you can add more if you like.

- ✓ *ummm*
- ✓ *ahhh*
- ✓ *uhhh*
- ✓ *so*
- ✓ *right*
- ✓ *you know*
- ✓ *like*
- ✓ *euh* (in French)
- ✓ *eto* or *ano* (Japanese)
- ✓ *esto* (Spanish)
- ✓ *jiege* (JEH-gu) (Mandarin)

And many, many more from around the world. As you can see, verbal crutches are not limited to American English speakers. The need to fill a silence is international in nature.

8.2.3 SPEECH

Pick any topic you like for your speech. **Pick quickly** so you can begin writing and practicing as soon as possible. However, take a 'little' time to **make sure it is something you are excited about or know very well**.

We talked about how you should "**talk to your audience**" rather than perform a script for them? This is where that really begins to show.

Because the audience will be counting your verbal crutches, you'll want to know your topic well enough to **talk about it as you would to a friend**. When you're having a conversation, you **don't** usually stop in the middle and think, "*Let's see, what had I planned to say here?*"

During a conversation, **one point leads to the next and you just keep moving**. That's the way a speech should be.

So, pick your topic and **let's write your speech**:

1. <u>Outline</u> your speech starting with opening and closing points.

2. Start filling in the very middle. Remember, only short bullet points and thoughts for now. You'll fill in all the detail later.

3. You have a beginning, a middle, and an end. Now start filling in all the points you want in between.

4. Once you have a good list of points in the proper place in your outline, then you can start filling in detail.

Remember! **Do not write your speech word-for-word.** Most people do not write the same way they speak. That's a skill we'll work on later. For now, you'll want to capture the points and details you need, but **the actual words and sentences you'll speak will come from you, from your passion, not from the paper.**

8.3   PRACTICE

Since the Exercise requires no practice, we'll concentrate on your speech. You might be a little concerned that you will not know your speech well enough to give it without notes. That's okay.

Remember your exercise on "**what's the worst that could happen?**" **Nothing really bad happened, right**? Well, the worst that could happen here is that you would forget your point or get lost and not remember what to say for a moment.

> There! Now I won't be tempted to say "ummm" too many times.

Is the audience going to boo? **No!** Are they going to stampede and trample you? **No!** Are they going to laugh at you and throw pie in your face? **No!** Are they going to be supportive and wait patiently while you get back on track? **Yes!** They might even help you.

The one thing they *will definitely* be doing is **counting any verbal fillers you use**. This could result in you having to give your speech twice. THAT'S the worst that could happen. *Not so bad, eh?*

So, let's see what you can do to overcome any tendency to use these verbal crutches to fill silence as you practice.

1. **Realize Silence is Okay:** A few moments of silence while you think or recover is okay. You don't have to fill it with "something." *In fact, you can embrace it and <u>use it for emphasis</u>.*

2. **Practice Out Loud:** We recommend this throughout this course for a reason. It helps you get comfortable with what you intend to say. Visualizing the result is easier if you've actually done it a few times.

3. **Know Your Speech**: If you know your topic inside and out, or at the very least are very excited about it. Remember the last time you got very excited about something (a new toy, a new game, this Gabberz program)? Nobody could get you to shut up about it for days. That's the kind of excitement you want.

4. **Use Good Notes, Not a Script**: If you try to follow a script, your mind will try to remember it basically word-for-word. This greatly increases the potential for pauses where verbal fillers can slip in.

5. **Memorize the Introduction**: We have been telling you not to memorize your speech. However, if you have your short opening lines down comfortably stone-cold, that will give you confidence right at the start and help get your momentum going. It doesn't need to be word-for-word, you just need to be very comfortable jumping right into the first part.

6. **Connect with the Audience**: See how it's all starting to come together? Make eye contact; engage with your audience; smile at them. All this makes it easier to be conversational and have your speech flow easily.

7. **Record/Listen to Your Practices**: If you're up to it, record your practices and listen to them. Try to identify the verbal crutches you use and eliminate them.

There are many other ways to help banish verbal crutches from your speaking patterns. If you have a few, that's okay; we'll keep working throughout the program to help you minimize or banish them.

So don't get too upset or bothered if you have some. Most people do. Recognizing them is half the battle.

8.4 PRESENT

It's almost time for your speech event. We had told you not to use any scripts or notes. If you're really concerned, you can use a couple of 3x5 note cards with a few bullet points. But that's it! No paragraphs. No sentences. Just a single word or two for each of your top 10 points.

Finally, review the **Do/Do Not Table** for a quick list of the things you'll want to do vs. the things you should avoid.

DO/DO NOT TABLE Lesson 4	
DO	**DO NOT**
• **WAIT SILENTLY FOR SILENCE TO PASS.** • Smile and gesture. • Look your audience in the eye and have a conversation with them. • If you get lost, confused, or just plain forget, smile and keep silent until the moment passes. • Be animated, cheerful, excited. • Introduce yourself at beginning and thank the audience at end. • Have fun!	• **DO NOT FILL A SILENCE WITH ANY SOUND!** • Do not stop and restart if you make a mistake or forget. **Just keep going no matter what.** • **Do not apologize** for making a mistake or forgetting. • Do not be bland and monotone. • Do not fear forgetfulness, the moment will pass. • You do not need to be perfect.

8.5   SPEECH TIME

Now it's time to get ready for the speech. We'll prepare your audience, get you introduced, and get you on "stage" for your exercise and speech. Are you prepared to videotape your event?

8.5.1   AUDIENCE PREPARATION

You or someone you assign should bring the audience into your "auditorium" and seat them in the proper place for your speech. The audience should be given instructions similar to the following once they are seated (the announcer should have fun with verbal tics).

ANNOUNCER

- *"**Ummm**... Welcome and, **uh**, thank you for attending, **ummm**, attending - Student's Name - speech for, **like**, **you know**, Level 1, of **ummm**, Lesson 4. Your, **you know**, participation is, **like**, critical to the, **uhhh**, success of the, **ah**, the, **you know**, the training.*

- *Obviously, today's topic is about those pesky little verbal crutches and fillers like **ummm**, **you know**, and **like**.*

- *- Student's Name - will be out shortly and he will lead us in a short little game to help us focus on these fillers.*

- *After that, the Student will give a 3 to 4 minute speech.*

- *Your job during the speech will be to keep track of the number of times the Student uses any verbal crutches to fill a silence.*

- *Silence is okay. But you want to capture every time the Student resorts to **ummm, ahhh, like**, or any other crutch to fill that silence or pause.*

- *If the Student accumulates more than 20 of these during the speech, he will need to give the speech a second time and try to improve that score.*

- *Don't worry, he/she can only give the speech twice.*

- *Now, Ladies and, **ummm**, Gentlemen, it's time for the, **uh**, **like**, speech. With a round of applause, I'd like you to welcome, **ummm, you know, - Student's Name .**"*

Use your imagination or embellish the introduction if you like. If there are multiple students, do the introductions for each other. If there is only one student and a small audience, you can do the instructions and introduction yourself (with appropriate adjustments). Try and make this an "event" for everyone.

8.5.2 STUDENT PREPARATION

By now, you should be ready and excited about getting out there and doing your speech.

- You have practiced enough to know your material well.

- You have **eliminated your reliance on using your notes while practicing** (if you keep relying on your notes during practice, it will be hard to go without them during your event).

- Your audience is seated.

- Maybe you've given them a list of the verbal crutches to be looking for during your speech.

- The video camera is charged up and ready to go. Either it is on a tripod or someone in your audience is ready to tape your event.

And now... it's speech time !

8.5.3 LESSON 4 EXERCISE/SPEECH

IF YOU EVER GET LOST, COME BACK HERE FOR STEP-BY-STEP INSTRUCTIONS.

This is "generally" how your event should go. If things go different, that's okay. This is just a suggested guide.

THE EXERCISE, STEP-BY-STEP!

8.5.3.1 EXERCISE GAME – THE LONG UMMMMMMM...

1. As soon as you're introduced, step in front of your audience, look them in the eyes, and smile.

2. Give your audience a reminder on how the Exercise Game works. *"First, we're going to play a little game. I'm going to pick a verbal filler for us. Then, on the count of three, I want everyone to take a deep breath and say the sound as long as you can, like this... 'ummmmmm'. The last one sounding wins!"*

3. Then you pick a sound. If you use something such as "**like**", have them repeat it quickly over-and-over in a single breath. Give the sound, count to three, and do it... keep going.

4. Now, take a deep breath, and say, *"That was great. You (point to winner) win. Would you like to do another sound?"*

5. If they say yes, pick a new sound. We don't recommend going for more than three unless everyone's having a bunch of fun.

6. Thank your audience for their participation and let them know it's time to get into the speech.

THE SPEECH, STEP-BY-STEP!

8.5.3.2 SPEECH – THE UMMM CRUNCHER

7. Remind your audience what they need to do during your speech (also be sure that they have **paper and pens**, or some way of recording the number of fillers you use). Say...

   *"Now, I am going to give a speech and try **NOT** to use any verbal crutches. I need you to listen carefully and keep a tally of the number of times I use ANY crutch. If, at the end, I've got more than 20, I'll need to give the speech again and try to reduce that number. Are you ready?"*

8. Take a deep breath, get your wonderful opening in your mind, smile, and begin.

9. Make an effort to **entertain your audience with a fun and exciting speech.** Remember to accept silent pauses as an opportunity to add emphasis or character to your speech—not to use verbal fillers to hide them.

Go forth. Speak clearly. **Be a proud Gabberz!**

8.6 ANALYSIS & SCORING

These are your **Analysis and Scoring Sheets** for this lesson.

ANALYSIS & SCORING SHEETS – LESSON 4

INSTRUCTIONS FOR AUDIENCE SCORING:

Audience Members: please work together to score the speaker honestly in the identified categories.

AUDIENCE: Rank the following categories from 1 to 5 where: 1 = Needs Work/Strongly Disagree 5 = Excellent/Strongly Agree	**1 to 5**
The Speaker completed an exercise where he/she led the audience in a game.	
The Speaker appeared to be in charge of the game.	
The Speaker gave clear instructions for both the game and what the audience needed to do for the speech.	
The Speaker gave a 3 to 4 minute speech and used verbal crutches less than 20 times.	
The Speaker gave a 3 to 4 minute speech and used verbal crutches more than 20 times and had to give the speech a second time.	
The Speaker clearly knew most of the material in the speech, even if some portions of it were forgotten.	
The Speaker varied voice and tone to make the speech interesting.	
Comments:	

SELF-ASSESSMENT BY THE STUDENT:

Please rank yourself fairly so you can see how you improve over time.

STUDENT: Rank the following categories from 1 to 5 where: 1 = Needs Work/Strongly Disagree 5 = Excellent/Strongly Agree	1 to 5
The audience did not turn into an angry mob and chase me down with pitchforks and torches.	
I was not embarrassed doing the game or the speech.	
I felt like I knew what I wanted to say while I was giving the speech.	
I was aware of it whenever I used one of the verbal crutches.	
I tried to keep silent whenever I felt the urge to use a verbal crutch.	
(If a 2nd speech was needed) I found it was easier on the second speech to use fewer verbal crutches.	
I felt prepared and ready when the time came.	
I had fun and enjoyed leading the game and giving the speeches.	
I understood the directions and instructions for this lesson and had no problem completing the task.	
I had a lot of fun doing this exercise and lesson.	
Comments:	

8.7 CONGRATULATIONS! PREPARE FOR LESSON 5

Congratulations on completing yet another lesson. You are well on your way to developing powerful speaking skills.

Here are a few things you need to do to prepare for Lesson 5.

- **FIRST!** Thank everyone for their support and let them know that you have another speech in about **1 week**. Yikes! That's right, only 1 week to prepare.

- When that's done, **take a deep breath and relax**. But not too much, you need to practice for Lesson 5.

- The good news is that you won't be doing any writing for Lesson 5. We've done all the speech prep for you.

www.gabberz.com

Gabberz Public Speaking for Kids, Tweens, and Teens
Level 1, Single-Student, Do-it-Yourself

CHAPTER 9

LESSON 5—VOICE CONTROL

What You'll Learn in This Chapter:

✓ How to breath properly.

✓ How to project your voice.

✓ How to speak with conviction.

✓ Voice is 38% of comprehension.

9 LESSON 5—VOICE CONTROL

9.1 OVERVIEW

9.1.1 INTRODUCTION

SUGGESTION !
Remember to read <u>all</u> of Chapter 9 first, then go back to Section 9.2.2 to do the lesson.

Your voice is a flexible instrument that you must learn to use properly in order to gain the desired effect on your audience. Whether speaking to 1 person or 1000, your voice (**as opposed to your words**) will play a large part in how much your audience cares about and understands what you are saying.

Your **voice** can convey *confidence* and *conviction*—or it can convey *weakness* and a *lack of moral character*. **The good news is that you have complete control over this.** You are the one who will shape your audience's vision of who you are.

Here's the Overview Table for this lesson:

Lesson 5 Overview	
Preparation Time	**1 Week**
Schedule	Date _____ Day _____ Time _____
Lesson	You'll read a speech we've written for you. You will need to read it twice. The first time will be flat with no emotion. The second time will be with exaggerated emotion and voice.
Exercise	Gabberz-provided speech in **Appendix C**. This is a reading of the speech. But you **must** read it with a **very flat, emotionless** voice.
Speech	The same speech in **Appendix C**. This time, you will **read it with exaggerated emotion** and you must **follow the noise cues** provided in the speech (you'll understand shortly).
Goals	You will learn the power and control your voice can command when used properly.

9.1.2 YOUR VOICE SPEAKS VOLUMES ABOUT YOU

9.1.2.1 GENERAL

When we talk about "voice" here, we're talking about **much more than just how you sound or how loudly you speak**. Your "voice" is made up of lots of little things that add up to a big picture of you.

- Is your voice authentic and genuine? Are you?

- Is it strong and resonant? Or weak and breathy?

- Do you sound relaxed and comfortable?

- Do you speak too fast? Or jumble/mumble the words?

- Is your voice warm and pleasant? Or frazzled and tense?

- Do you have a nasal voice or a gravelly voice?

- Do you use too many words, thinking that quantity equals quality? (Tip... no, it does not!)

- Is your voice flat and emotionless? Or is it full of passion, emotion, and a genuine desire to share with your audience?

Does my voice look okay?

All of these things are critical to how you present yourself and how your audience perceives the quality of your words. The proper voice can help your audience believe you are **honest, genuine, and passionate with a firm belief in what you are talking about**. Fail to control your voice and your audience *might* think of you as shallow, untrustworthy, or unbelievable. Or, at the very least, difficult to understand.

This lesson will **begin to lay the groundwork** for how you can develop a powerful, resonant, and authentic voice that demands the attention and respect of your audience. This will not all happen in this lesson, but we'll start **tuning your instrument** now and preparing you to be a powerful speaker.

9.1.2.2 PROJECTION?

Many people believe that, if someone says, *"we can't hear you,"* that it simply means they should just speak louder.

But, that's not it at all. Have you ever been at a party or family gathering where someone was speaking and **their voice seemed to fill the room**? They appeared to be speaking normally, but when they spoke, their voice cut through the background noise and demanded attention.

Yeah, but a breath mint wouldn't hurt!

Those people have command of their voice!

Public Speaking for Kids, Tweens, and Teens – Confidence for Life!

Gabberz®

You may also have heard others speaking in that same room who could not be understood over the din of chatter around them. No matter how loudly the speaker raised their voice, people struggled to understand what they were saying.

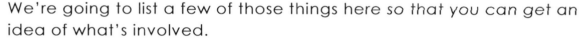

There's **more going on here than volume**. And that's what we're going to *begin* working on in this lesson.

9.1.2.3 WHAT MAKES A POWERFUL VOICE?

There are many different elements that make up a **powerful, authentic, and pleasing voice**. We're going to list a few of those things here *so that you can get an* idea of what's involved.

Good news! You **don't** have to memorize this list, or even remember all of it. We will work on some this now during this lesson. The rest will be covered in other lessons throughout the program, or you can do your own research.   This lesson is only a start. If you work at it, by the end of this program, **you will have a commanding and powerful voice**.

Some elements that make up that commanding and powerful voice are:

- **Confidence and conviction**. If *you* are unsure or unconvinced yourself, that will be visible in your voice. Watch how people speak in normal conversation. You'll quickly learn to spot the difference between someone who is absolutely convinced in what they're saying, and when someone is unsure or uncertain.

- **Being honest, being yourself**. As we've said throughout, **you must be absolutely honest**—not only in what you say, but in who you are. Do not put on a false front. Just be yourself, that's who people will listen to.

- **Passion and emotion**. A deadpan voice and emotionless face will dampen your voice and kill your ability to maintain the interest of your audience. Your audience wants to feel what you feel—give them that opportunity.

Take a deeeeep breath...

- **Breathing properly**. Breathing and breath control are vital to your ability to be a powerful speaker. Shallow breathing (throat, top of chest) gives you a thin, weak, or harsh voice. Belly (or diaphragmatic) breathing gives you full vocal control. We will work on methods to breathe properly throughout the program, but for now, we'll just start you off with a little primer and exercise in **Section 9.1.2.5**.

- **An easy, natural voice**. Your voice is a **fine instrument**. Just like playing a guitar or piano, the more you practice with it, the more natural it sounds. The advantage we have is that everyone knows how to play the "voice," they just may not play it well. Don't force yourself into anything unnatural, just relax, be yourself, and practice these techniques at every opportunity.

- **Mask Resonance**. *Don't worry about this right now*. We just wanted to introduce you to the term. "**Mask Resonance**" is like the natural echo chamber in your face. Resonance gives your voice charisma and strength. You can do research on your own if you like, but we'll work on this later.

- **Relaxation**. Relax. Prepare and practice and you'll do fine. Remember to turn nervousness to your advantage. This will help you find that fine balance between relaxation and energy.

- **Pacing**. Energy, variety, pauses, speed, slow talking, fast talking, etc. All of these have a variable impact your audience.

- **Inflection**. This is a fun one. The words you emphasize when speaking can change the meaning of the words dramatically. Be careful, but learn to use it to your advantage. Try the fun exercise in **Section 9.1.2.4** below.

Now *that's* one handsome guy!

There are many more elements that can impact your voice and how your "words" are perceived. Some studies have shown that 38% of perception, comprehension, and acceptance comes from vocal factors (voice), while only 7% comes from the actual words we say. (The remaining 55% comes from visuals such as body language, appearance, etc.)

9.1.2.4 INFLECTION

Inflection is critical to communication and comprehension. To see how this works, we'll repeat the same sentence seven times, providing the <u>**emphasis**</u> on a different word each time.

Read each sentence below out loud. Each time, **strongly** emphasize the bold underlined word. Note how the meaning changes.

- <u>*I*</u> never said he stole the money.

- I <u>***never***</u> said he stole the money.

- I never <u>***said***</u> he stole the money.

- I never said <u>***he***</u> stole the money.

- I never said he <u>***stole***</u> the money.

- I never said he stole <u>***the***</u> money.

- I never said he stole the <u>***money***</u>.

See how the meaning changes each time. *"Who" said it? Was it "said"? Did "he" steal the money? Was "money" even stolen?* **Context** and **inflection** are incredibly powerful tools. Use them wisely. Use them only for good, not for evil.

9.1.2.5 BREATHING

Breathing is, of course, essential to life. Proper breathing is essential to a powerful voice. Here's a simple exercise to get you started on the path.

1. Sit upright in a chair and relax your stomach muscles.

2. Breathe in deeply through your nose. Fill yourself from the bottom up starting with your abdomen (**your stomach should expand, not your ribs**). *Then*, as you fill, you can expand your ribs. Continue until you are filled with air from your abdomen to your chin.

3. Hold your breath for five to ten seconds.

4. Exhale slowly **starting by tightening your abdominal muscles** to push the air up and out. Keep your ribs expanded so the air comes from your abdomen first.

5. Start slowly. Repeat on a regular basis. Eventually, you'll be able to incorporate proper breathing naturally into your speaking.

9.1.3   GOALS

You have one simple (but powerful) goal for this lesson.

* **Goal 1:** Learn that proper control of your **voice** gives you confidence, maintains the attention of your audience, and helps guide them to full understanding and comprehension of what you are trying to communicate.

9.2   PREPARE

9.2.1   WHAT YOU'LL BE DOING

Now, let's see what you'll be doing in Lesson 5.

What You'll Be Doing – LESSON 5	
What	You will be reading a speech we've written for you. You will read it **twice**. Although it is the same speech, **it will be very different each time**.
When	Date _____ Day _____ Time _____
Who	Try to schedule your speech with **as many people as possible**. These speeches are always more fun with more people.
Where	Your audience will not be interacting directly with you on this speech so they can be seated anywhere. They should be seated facing you while you stand at an appropriate distance where everyone can see and hear you clearly.
Prepare	No preparation is required for this lesson. The speech is written for you. You should familiarize yourself with the speech prior to your event. You don't need to memorize it, you can read it during your event.
EXERCISE — Lesson 5	
What?	You will find your prepared speech in **Appendix C**, you'll read the introduction page to the audience, and then read the speech. For this exercise, you will read the speech with NO emotion, in a flat voice, and you will not follow the vocal directions in the speech. See **Section 9.2.2** for more information.
Length?	2 to 3 minute speech read at normal speaking speed.

Public Speaking for Kids, Tweens, and Teens – Confidence for Life!

SPEECH — Lesson 5

What?	The SAME Gabberz-provided speech in **Appendix C**. You'll read the same speech, but this time, you'll use **exaggerated** emotion and follow the **vocal Instructions** provided in the speech.
Length?	2 to 3 minute speech read at normal speaking speed.
Note	1. Take a few minutes between the exercise and the speech to familiarize yourself with the vocal Instructions in the speech.

9.2.2 EXERCISE—STONEWALL

This exercise will be easy for some people (maybe even natural), but may be harder for others to do properly. We have provided a complete speech for you to use so there is no preparation required.

COME BACK HERE **AFTER** YOU'VE **READ** THE ENTIRE CHAPTER.

Here's what you must do.

1. Go right now and read the cover page to the speech in **Appendix C**. You can also go ahead and read the speech now.

2. When it's time for your event, you will do *this* exercise first.

3. You will read the Audience cover note first, then you will read the speech as described below.

4. This exercise is simply a bland, emotionless, flat reading of the text in the speech. Simple! (Or is it?)

You might call this "**anti-exaggeration**." Your goal will be to read this entire speech in as flat a voice as you can with absolutely no variation in tone, emotion, or facial cues. Don't smile, don't laugh, don't make eye contact. Speak in a monotone.

In fact, we're asking you to break every rule we've talked about. **Make your speech as boring as possible and do your best to put your audience to sleep**.

IMPORTANT: For the exercise portion of this lesson, do **NOT** follow the vocal directions that you'll see in the speech. Also, do not read those out loud. Those are for your next reading.

9.2.3 SPEECH—WAKE THEM UP!

Now that you've put your audience to sleep, it's time to wake them up for the fun part. You are going to read them the same speech, but this time, you'll add your "**voice**" to it.

Here's what you need to do:

1. After you have done the exercise described previously, you'll take a **short** break and come back to read your speech again.

2. Do **not** read the vocal directions [the words in brackets in red] out loud during your speech, you will only act on them as directed.

MOST IMPORTANT: Regardless of the Vocal Directions (which should help you with voice control and proper breathing), **you MUST put as much emotion and animation into the speech as you can**.

Tell the story as if you'd lived it. **Act it out.** Be animated in such a way that it demands the attention of your audience.

As you're doing all this, watch how differently your audience reacts between this reading and the exercise you did before. The <u>words</u> are the same. The <u>story</u> is the same. **Only <u>YOU</u> are different.**

If you'd like to do it again, just let your audience know you'd like to try again so you can get more emotion into it. I'm sure they'll be happy to do that.

9.3 PRACTICE

No practice is necessary for either the exercise or the speech. You'll be reading the speech we prepared for you during your exercise, then again during the speech. We do recommend that familiarize yourself with the **Vocal Directions** and prepare yourself to make the most of those ahead of time.

9.4 PRESENT

It's almost time for your speech event. Here are a few final notes before the big show.

1. A couple of days before your speech, verify that everyone who has agreed to come remembers the event and still plans to attend.

2. The day of the event, double-check to make sure you have everything you need. In this case, it's just a copy of the speech you'll be using.

Finally, review the **Do/Do Not Table** for a quick list of the things you'll want to do vs. the things you should avoid. Don't worry if you do some do not's or do not do some do's.

DO/DO NOT TABLE	
Lesson 5	
DO	**DO NOT**
• Stand tall and straight. • Keep going, even if you mess up. • Be animated, cheerful, excited (except during the exercise). • Make a real effort to act out the speech. • Breathe properly and deeply. • Have fun!	• Do not stop and restart if you make a mistake or forget. **Just keep going no matter what.** • **Do not apologize** for making a mistake or forgetting. • Do not fear the Vocal Directions. Embrace them. • You do not need to be perfect.

9.5 SPEECH TIME

We **highly recommend** that you record your exercise and speech for this lesson. Afterwards, you can review them and compare the impact that the **bland reading** of the speech has versus the **high-impact reading** in the exercise. The audience is yours to command. You can either put them to sleep, or draw them into your world. You choose.

9.5.1 AUDIENCE PREPARATION

Your audience will not have a roll in this event other than to sit back and enjoy your speeches. You can tell them that you'll be giving the same speech twice in different ways, BUT, don't tell them what that difference is. You want them to come to their own conclusions.

When it is time for your speech event, someone you assign should bring the audience into your "auditorium" and seat them in the proper place for your speech. **The Announcer should give the audience instructions similar to the following** once they are seated:

- *"Welcome and thank you for attending* <u>- Student's Name -</u> *speech for Level 1, Lesson 5. Your participation is critical to success with the* **Gabberz Speech Training Program***.*

- *You will not have a roll in this event, other than to sit back and enjoy.*

- <u>- Student's Name -</u> *will be out shortly and tell a 2 to 3 minute story.*

- *After a short break,* <u>- Student's Name -</u> *will come back out to tell the same story in a slightly different way.*

- *Now, Ladies and Gentlemen, it's time for the speech. With a round of applause, I'd like you to welcome* <u>- Student's Name -</u>*."*

9.5.2 STUDENT PREPARATION

There's not much you can do to prepare for this one other than the breathing exercise we told you about (you are doing that, aren't you?).

- You have your speech package in hand.

- Your audience is seated.

- They've been given instructions.

- You should start the video camera during the introduction so you have the whole event captured. Make sure it's pointed in the right place for you.

And now... it's speech time !

9.5.3 LESSON 5 EXERCISE/SPEECH

You'll be doing the exercise first, and then you'll be do the speech after a **short** break.

THE EXERCISE, STEP-BY-STEP!

9.5.3.1 EXERCISE – STONEWALL

1. After the introduction, step up in front of your audience (and position for the camera if necessary).

2. Smile at the audience and thank the "Announcer."

3. Find the **Audience Letter** and read that to them.

4. Flip the page. Take a good, deep, **abdominal breath**. And read.

5. Remember—<u>no</u> emotion, <u>no</u> inflection, just <u>flat monotone</u>. **DO NOT** read the **BOLD** instructions out loud.

6. When you finish, tell them you'll be taking a moment to prepare for the speech portion and will let them know when you are ready.

7. Leave the room and take a moment to review the speech and prepare to follow the Vocal Directions given in the speech.

THE SPEECH, STEP-BY-STEP!

9.5.3.2 SPEECH – WAKE THEM UP!

1. Let your "Announcer" know you are ready. The Announcer will step up say something like, "*Ladies and Gentlemen, please give a round of applause for our next speaker,   Student's Name   *".

2. Smile at the audience and thank the "Announcer" by name.

3. Hold up the speech very theatrically and say something like, "***Let's see what's going to happen this time, shall we***?"

4. Do **not** read the **Audience Letter** again.

5. **DO NOT** read the **BOLD** instructions out loud.

6. Take a good, deep, **abdominal breath**. And read.

7. Remember—this time you will tell the story with **great, exaggerated emotion**, interjecting the sounds/words as instructed by the Vocal Directions. **Be very animated, loud, and excited.**

8. Breathe properly and use your **voice** to draw your audience into the story. **Have fun with it.** Your audience wants to have fun, do your best to give them that.

9. When you finish, bow and take your applause.

Go forth. Speak clearly. Be a proud Gabberz!

9.6 ANALYSIS & SCORING

We hope you had a lot of fun with this lesson. It may not seem like you did much, but there were a lot of foundational techniques built into this simple reading:

- proper breathing,

- voice control,

- tone, character, emotion,

- audience engagement.

Most importantly, you should have seen for yourself the difference it makes in "**how**" the material is presented. Although the words and the story were the same both times, they were vastly different in how they were presented.

We can "tell" you how this is different all we want, but you need to experience it.

- Did **you** feel differently between the exercise and the speech?

- Did your audience react differently each time?

- Were they more, or less, engaged?

- Which speech did they *like* better?

Most importantly, once again, you were able to get up in front of an audience and tell a story. That's a great accomplishment. You're well on your way to earning your place as a *Gabberz Master Speaker*.

Below is your **Scoring Sheet** for this lesson. **Hand the scoring sheet to your audience as soon as you have completed your speech event.**

Your **Self-Assessment Checklist** follows that. You should complete that yourself as soon as the event is over while the event is still fresh in your mind. Try to be honest with yourself.

ANALYSIS & SCORING SHEETS – LESSON 5

INSTRUCTIONS FOR AUDIENCE SCORING:

Audience Members: please work together to score the speaker in the identified categories. Please provide honest input to help the speaker identify both strong and weak skills.

AUDIENCE: Rank the following categories from 1 to 5 where: 1 = Needs Work/Strongly Disagree 3 = Average/Agree 5 = Excellent/Strongly Agree	1 to 5
The Speaker appeared interested and excited about doing this event.	
The Speaker read the speech at least twice. The first time with **no** emotion, the second time with emotion and character.	
We found the second speech much more interesting than the first monotone exercise.	
The Speaker interjected unexpected sounds, words, or vocalizations within the second speech.	
During the second speech, the Speaker varied voice, tone, emotion, etc.	
The Speaker appeared to have enough breath and control to speak clearly and loud enough for the audience to hear.	
Although the Speaker was required to read from a prepared speech, the Speaker looked at or engaged with the audience from time-to-time.	
The Speaker smiled during the speech.	
Comments:	

SELF-ASSESSMENT BY THE STUDENT:

Please rank yourself fairly so that you can see how you improve over time.

STUDENT: Rank the following categories from 1 to 5 where: 1 = Needs Work/Strongly Disagree 5 = Excellent/Strongly Agree	1 to 5
Nobody watered me down with a fire hose.	
I was not embarrassed doing the exercise.	
I was not embarrassed giving the speech.	
The speech was easier to give than the exercise.	
The speech was more fun than the exercise.	
I was comfortable conveying strong emotion.	
I was comfortable following the Vocal Directions.	
I had fun and enjoyed giving the speeches.	
The breathing exercises helped me during the speech.	
I understood the directions and instructions for this lesson and had no problem completing the task.	
I learned that this is not hard to do.	
I am having fun doing these exercises and speeches.	
Comments:	

9.7 CONGRATULATIONS! PREPARE FOR LESSON 6

Congratulations on completing this lesson. I'm sure you did a great job and you're one step closer to becoming a *Gabberz Master Speaker*.

Here are a few things you need to do to prepare for Lesson 6.

- **Take a deep breath and relax**. But not too much, there's work to be done for Lesson 6.

- You'll need to write a speech for the next lesson, but <u>don't worry</u>, the content won't matter that much.

www.gabberz.com

Gabberz Public Speaking for Kids, Tweens, and Teens
Level 1, Single-Student, Do-it-Yourself

CHAPTER 10

LESSON 6—BODY LANGUAGE

SUGGESTION !
To help you understand the lesson better, we suggest you read <u>all</u> of Chapter 10 first before you do any work, then go back to Section 10.2.2 and begin working through the lesson.

What You'll Learn in This Chapter:

✓ Your body is an instrument.

✓ How to stand and move.

✓ What to do with your hands.

✓ Body language is 55% of audience comprehension.

10 LESSON 6—BODY LANGUAGE

10.1 OVERVIEW

10.1.1 INTRODUCTION

We've talked about how **your voice is an instrument**—so too is your body. Your body tells a lot of tales without you even knowing it. If your body language doesn't match what you're saying, it sends all kinds of **distracting** and **conflicting** signals to your audience.

In this lesson, we'll learn what **"body language"** is, how important it is in communication, and how it influences your audience.

Don't hate me...

This lesson is longer than usual, but it's <u>very</u> important.

Try to hang in there!

Lesson 6 Overview	
Preparation Time	**2 Weeks**
Schedule	Date _____ Day _____ Time _____
Lesson	You will write a speech for this lesson and give it twice under two very different scenarios.
Exercise	In this exercise, your audience will pose you in different positions while you give your speech.
Speech	You'll give the same speech, but this time your audience will give you some actions, movements, or dances.
Goals	You will learn how "body language" affects your audience; how to move & speak fluidly; and how to be comfortable standing in front of your audience.

10.1.2 SPEAKING WITH BODY LANGUAGE

10.1.2.1 WHY IS "BODY LANGUAGE" IMPORTANT?

Have you ever wondered why you suddenly start to distrust someone or firmly believe they are lying—without even knowing why you're feeling that way? Why do you feel comfort and trust in someone you've just met? Or dislike someone else almost instantly.

Frequently, this happens because **you are unconsciously (or subconsciously) picking up on the person's *body language*.** Little clues in their face, the way they stand, what they're doing with their hands, where they look, etc. can conflict with the words they are saying.

In general, **people are not persuaded by what we say**, but **rather by what they understand**! Put another way (with exceptions), "**it's not <u>what</u> you say, it's <u>how</u> you say it.**" Consider the following images and the phrase: "*I hate you.*"

"*I hate you.*" This is obviously anger related. The boy's body language (lowered eyebrows, closed body position, etc.) screams real anger. He means it.

"*I hate you.*" His body language (expression, open position, etc.) express a friendly jealousy. Maybe his best friend just got a great new bike or long board.

"*I hate you.*" Her body language (leaning in, intimate laugh, etc.) says that this is a joyful exchange between friends. Maybe her best friend just told the new boy in the choir that she liked him.

Same words, completely different meanings!

These three examples were pretty obvious. But there are thousands of large and small signs that we pick up on without conscious thought.

Think about a Mime... what do you see in the following picture? Is he happy, sad, angry, joyful? Or is he just a blank slate waiting to be read?

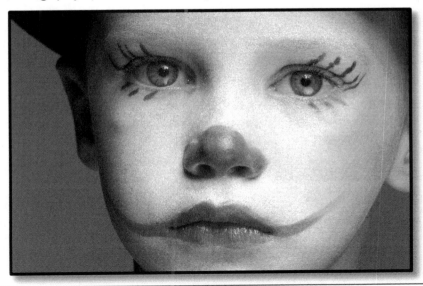

A good Mime can convey complex emotions, provide detailed imagery, and tell entire stories **without saying a single word**. How does he do that? It's done with **a thorough understanding of how body language conveys meaning**.

10.1.2.2 WHAT IS "BODY LANGUAGE"?

So, what is body language? It is made up of many elements that all come together to paint a complete picture of the person and what they are saying.

Is it always accurate? Not necessarily (see the next section on reading body language). But in most cases, it helps us understand what is being said, the context, and maybe even how we should feel about it.

Here are a few of things that make up what we call body language:

- eye contact,
- voice,
- facial expression,
- posture,
- movement,
- gestures,
- how you stand (stance),
- hands and feet,
- where you look,
- and much more.

Have we mentioned lately that you <u>DON'T</u> have to memorize any of this?

Zzzzzz... eyes... look left? hands... wringing... posture...

When body language conflicts with words, **the unconscious mind can be very persuasive** in convincing us to believe in a way that is in direct contradiction to those words. Throughout this program, we'll see what a tremendous impact this has on our communications.

10.1.2.3 READING BODY LANGUAGE

The importance of the <u>**unconscious**</u> (or subconscious) **reading** of body language cannot be overstated. Many studies have been done regarding body language, but a commonly accepted rule of thumb is the "*3 V's Rule*".

3 V's Rule

According to some studies, people's perception, comprehension, and feelings about a speaker are gathered from these 3 factors:

1. **VISUAL** = **55%** (body language, appearance, etc.)

2. **VOCAL** = **38%** (tone, timbre, inflection)

3. **VERBAL** = **7%** (the actual words that were said)

Having said all of that, keep in mind that **conscious** (or on purpose) interpretation of someone's body language is more of an **art than a science**. It must encompass many different data points—most of which can be tricked or faked.

There's all kinds of advice out there about how to "read" body language. **Be careful**. "Paint-by-Number" or "Point-and-Click" advice abounds. These "techniques" *claim* to easily identify when someone is lying or hiding something. If you were to act on the belief that someone is lying because they looked up and to the left when they answered a question, **there's a high probability that you could be wrong**. That could create a bad situation.

However, if you begin to understand what body language *can* tell you, you begin to understand what signals you are sending. This gives you an advantage in building understanding and comprehension when you speak.

10.1.2.4 TIPS AND HINTS

So, how do you put body language to use for you?

Do you like my natural smile?

The more you understand how your body language unconsciously affects others, the more you can control it to match your message. You're not learning how to lie with body language, but how **to enhance your message and prevent body language from conflicting with words**.

Before we get into the lesson, here are a few tips for you. We could give thousands, but this is enough for now.

- <u>Smile</u>: *Smile and the whole world smiles with you.* **Never underestimate the importance of smiling**. Smile when you get in front of your audience, and keep smiling (where appropriate) until you leave. Have we mentioned lately that you should smile?

- <u>Be Natural</u>: As with all the advice we give you, don't try to force anything. **Be natural**. **Be yourself**. When you try to fake it, people will see that. Learn to be comfortable and natural with yourself.

- <u>Eye Contact</u>: Maintain that **visual connection** with your audience. Look people in the eyes to let them know you are engaged and interested. Keep your eyes on them—moving around to different members to try and make them all feel like you're talking to them as individuals. **Give each enough attention to connect.**

- <u>Speak Directly</u>: Speak directly to your audience (whether one person or one hundred). Don't talk to your notes, your feet, or your PowerPoint presentation. **Speak to your audience** so they can feel the connection and you can read their reactions.

- <u>Open Posture/Gestures</u>: Later, we will learn more about open and closed postures and gestures. For now, just avoid closed gestures like arms crossed in front of you, the "fig leaf" stance (see next page), or pointing with a finger (point with an open palm instead). **Open postures and gestures mean you are more receptive** and make your audience more engaged and receptive in response.

- <u>Move Naturally</u>: Learn to move in **strong**, **controlled**, and **limited** motions. Each movement should have a **purpose** and be limited to what is necessary.

Public Speaking for Kids, Tweens, and Teens – Confidence for Life!

Gabberz®

- <u>Entrance</u>: Before you speak, you have to make your entrance. **Don't rush to start your speech!** Too many speakers make this mistake. You should walk to your spot; pause and smile at the audience; then, when their attention is on you, begin purposefully.

Really? What's wrong with this? I'm comfortable.

- <u>Stance</u>: Learn to be **at ease** in front of your audience. A defensive or uncertain stance can broadcast self-consciousness. You'll hear many stance terms throughout this program. These include the "**steeple**," the "**hand washer**," the "**huncher**," the "**leg crosser**," and the "**fig leaf position**." The fig leaf (hands clasped in front of your groin) is one of the most common weak stances. **Learn to stand tall, straight, and firm**, like a tree, but allow yourself to move fluidly.

- <u>Tiger-in-the-Cage</u>: Learn to move comfortably, using the whole space you've been given for your speech. **Command the space**, but don't let it become a crutch for nervous anxiety—or a fake attempt to create excitement. **Move purposefully before key points**, but *don't wander aimlessly—back-and-forth, back-and-forth—like a tiger.*

- <u>What Do I Do With My Hands?</u>: There's no easy answer. The most **neutral** position is with your hands hanging loosely at your sides. Many people find this hard to do, but **you can become comfortable with practice**. When singing at church, or standing in line, or any time you need to stand for any length of time, just hang your hands at your sides. It becomes natural after a while. Having said that, **you _don't_ want to give a speech with your hands just hanging at your sides for extended lengths of time**. Let's learn about "gesturing".

- <u>Hand Gestures</u>: Use your hands as a tool to help emphasize important points. Your audience remembers better when a point is attached to a specific action or movement. But **don't use excessive gestures** to the point where it's unnatural. Be comfortable gesturing so that **the gestures compliment your words**, not distract. And speaking of distractions...

- <u>**Repetitive Distractions**</u>: **Don't do it!** Anything that you do repetitively can easily become a distraction to some or all of your audience. **Once they fixate on your repetitive action, they quit listening** and start wondering, *"Why does he keep doing that?"* At that point, you've lost your audience. Repetitive distractions include anything you do more than 2 or 3 times that has no specific purpose. Examples include:

✓ Tapping fingers (or toes, or anything else),

✓ Rubbing your belly (or any part of your anatomy),

✓ Scratching your ear (or anything else),

✓ Picking your nose (enough said),

✓ Clucking your tongue (or any repetitive noise),

✓ Anything you repeat that doesn't have a purpose.

Oh, and did we mention that **you should smile a lot**?

We've covered some of these tips in previous lessons, and we'll continue to cover those and much more throughout the rest of this program.

10.1.3 GOALS

We could fill months of study working on body language—it's that important. However, for this lesson, we're just going to introduce you to the concept of body language and work on a couple of basic fundamentals.

We have two main goals for this lesson. Remember, we're still at the point where **you cannot do these lessons wrong**. As long as you do them, you have succeeded. However, **if you really embrace the lesson and give it your all, you'll get much more out of it for yourself**.

Here's what we want to accomplish in Lesson 6.

Ewwww, gross!

> **TIP !**
> Watch speeches by various people (politicians, actors, motivational speakers, etc.) and see if you can spot if their body language conflicts with what they're saying.

1. **Goal 1**: Your first goal is to learn to become more comfortable with your body while standing in front of an audience. You'll learn that your body is a part of your speaking tool set, and not an uncomfortable distraction.

2. **Goal 2**: You'll begin to learn how movement enhances OR detracts from your message. You'll also start learning how to move fluidly while speaking.

10.2 PREPARE

10.2.1 WHAT YOU'LL BE DOING IN LESSON 6

As usual, use this handy little table as an overview of the lesson.

OVERVIEW OF LESSON 6.

What You'll Be Doing – LESSON 6	
What	You'll do an exercise that involves you giving your speech (while your audience poses you in different positions). Then, you'll give the speech again (while your audience directs you in different movements). **You'll need to learn your speech well**.
When	Date _____ Day _____ Time _____
Who	Try to schedule your speech with **as many people as possible**. The larger your audience is, the more interaction there will be and the more fun it will be for everyone—including you!
Where	Your audience will be shouting directions while you are giving your speech, so you should be where you can see and hear them all clearly. Give yourself plenty of room to move!
Prepare	Some preparation will be required for this lesson. • You'll need to write a speech for this one. It should be simple and easy to remember. • You may want to prepare some suggestions for your audience for poses and action/dance moves. We'll provide more detail later. **VERY IMPORTANT**: You'll need to practice your speech to the point where **you can give it without referring to your notes**. We'll give you some tricks in the **Practice** section.
EXERCISE — Lesson 6	
What?	See **Section 10.2.3**. You'll do an exercise where you'll give your speech while your audience gives you different poses.
Length?	2 to 3 minute speech read at normal speaking speed. Time yourself during practice.

SPEECH — Lesson 6	
What?	See **Section 10.2.4.** You'll give your speech again while your audience directs you to act, move, dance, etc.
Length?	2 to 3 minute speech read at normal speaking speed. Time yourself during practice.
Notes	Although you can just ask your audience to make up poses, actions, and dances, you could also have them pick them from pieces of paper in a jar (or something like that). **Make it a kind of game for everyone.** You'll see how engaged your audience can become when you involve them.

COME BACK HERE AFTER YOU'VE READ THE ENTIRE CHAPTER.

10.2.2 WRITE YOUR SPEECH

You will need to write <u>one</u> speech that you will use in both the exercise and the speech portions of this lesson. **Write something that will be easy to remember** since it will be very hard for you to refer to any notes while speaking. Maybe a **structured topic/story** with a **logical flow** will help you to remember what to say. Come up with <u>your own speech idea</u>, but here are a few thoughts that might get you started:

- **A Guided Tour**: You play the role as a Tour Guide and take your audience through a tour of some place you know well (museum, aquarium, theme park, factory, etc.). A step-by-step tour will help you stay on track.

- **The Big Event**: Recall some big event that you are familiar with and walk your audience through what happened. Events might include a birthday, a celebration, the Spelling Bee, the big soccer win, or anything else you remember well.

- **The How-To**: Pick something you know how to do well, or can build, and give your audience a step-by-step guide on how you do it, or how they can do it.

Your speech does **NOT** have to be exciting or interesting (*although we **always** encourage excitement and interest*). Your audience will be engaged in making you do poses and actions, so may not be that engaged in the words you're saying. That's okay... *this time.*

And, **DON'T WORRY**, if you forget some of your speech or lose your place, that's okay. Take a quick look at your notes and keep going (we'll give some tips in the **Practice** section).

It's better if you can keep going to maintain momentum and interest, but this is <u>not</u> about memorizing your speech. You will gain some experience in recalling your speech, but that is not the goal here.

If you're having problems writing your speech, maybe these tips will help:

1. Go back and review **Chapter 3** on writing and ideas.

2. Come up with a topic quickly and begin writing. **Don't wait until the last minute.**

3. Remember the **Idea Book** we talked about earlier? If you've been keeping that up, maybe there's an idea in there for you.

4. **MOST IMPORTANT:** Get a topic and outline **quickly**... then just **start writing**.

10.2.3 EXERCISE—POSE ME LIKE A STATUE

This is a deceptively simple exercise. All you have to do is give your speech...

Okay, so maybe we never make it *that* simple. While you're giving your speech, **your audience will be yelling out statue poses** that you must shape your body into. Our goal here is to help you begin the process of becoming comfortable in your body while giving a speech in front of your audience.

And then I said, blah... blah... blah, blah, blah...

Here's how it works:

- You come out and begin giving your speech with your **arms hanging loosely at your sides**.

- Your audience has been instructed to **yell out statue poses** one-at-a time.

- After **two sentences**, you take the first pose. Give the next two sentences (<u>roughly</u>) in that pose.

"Stand like a big, giant X".

- Someone yells out **another pose** and you take that pose for about two sentences.

Public Speaking for Kids, Tweens, and Teens – Confidence for Life!

And so-on and so-on until your speech is done. Your mission is to give your speech as **clearly**, **cleanly**, and **fluidly** as you can while using your entire body to pose the statue as brilliantly as you can. <u>Don't skimp</u>. **Give your audience everything you've got and pose proudly!**

So, what about the poses? You can either leave it entirely to your audience and let them come up with whatever they can (*this **could be a lot of fun** as you'll have no idea what they're going to say*), OR, you can give them a list or a bunch of poses on slips of paper in a jar for them to pick from (***more like a game***). It's up to you.

Don't hurt yourself!

If you *want* to give your audience some ideas, here are a few.

Statue of Liberty	Stand on one leg	Kneel and touch your nose	Touch your toes
Twist your body as far as you can	Disco pose	Look out to sea (hand on brow)	Hug yourself tightly
Do your best Karate stance	Pose like a dog pointing	Stand like a big, giant "X"	Bend over backwards and face audience

The next step is to blah... blah... blah, blah. blah...

10.2.4 SPEECH

The Exercise portion is about **being still**. Your speech portion is now about **being fluid**. In both cases, it's about learning to give your speech in concert with your body.

This time, while you are giving your speech, **your audience will be yelling out motions and movements** that you must perform while giving your speech. Our goal here is to help you begin to build some comfort in your ability to move **purposefully** while speaking.

Here's how it works:

- You come out and begin giving your speech with your **arms hanging loosely at your sides**.

- Your audience has been instructed to **yell out various actions or movements for you to perform** one-at-a time.

"Fly like an airplane".

- After the first **two sentences**, begin the first action with exaggerated movements. Give approximately two sentences while performing that movement.

- Someone yells out **another action/movement** and you do that for about two sentences.

- And so-on and so-on until your speech is done.

MOST IMPORTANT: Try to maintain proper breathing so that you can speak clearly throughout your speech.

Your mission is to give your speech as **clearly**, **cleanly**, and **fluidly** as you can while performing the actions/movements as brilliantly as you can. **Don't skimp**. **Give them everything you've got!** They deserve it.

Same as with the poses, you can either leave the actions/movements entirely to your audience and let them come up with whatever they can OR you can give them a list or a bunch of actions cut up and put in a jar for them to pick from like a game. It's up to you.

Here are a few action ideas for this one.

Disco dance	Fly like an airplane	Do the "Twist" (dance)	Hop on one leg
Vibrate your whole body	Do the "Macarena"	Jumping Jacks	Teapot Pouring Tea
Run in place	Pretend Slow Motion Running	Chop Down a Tree	Lift Heavy Weights

10.3 PRACTICE

Practice for this speech is important because you won't be able to use much in the way of notes while posing and moving. This is why it's important to choose a speech with some of the following points in mind.

- It should be **something you know well**.

- It should be **something that has a logical flow** from point-to-point.

- It's helpful if it has a **physical step-by-step flow** like a museum tour or assembly/building of something.

Now that you have your speech, it's time to practice. Remember, you **never** want to "memorize" your speech. This makes it sound "canned," or "rehearsed," or like you are just reading words off a page.

Instead, you want to learn it well enough that you can **have a conversation with your audience** and address all the points you intend to make. A speech that you know well, but is spoken **off-the-cuff and in your own voice,** is generally accepted better and enjoyed by everyone.

Some tips for practicing and preparing for your exercise and speech.

1. **Know your Speech**: Read it, study it, learn the logical flow of it so you don't have to memorize... you just have to step through it.

2. **Practice Out Loud**: We've said this before. Silent rehearsal is only studying, it is NOT practicing. You must practice out loud at the volume you intend to speak during the actual event.

3. **Memorize your Introduction and Closing**: *In contrast to what we told you before,* you should have a firm grasp of your **first couple of opening lines** (this will get you started and into the flow) and your **last couple of closing lines** (to finish strong and clear).

4. **Use Good Notes to Practice**: Once you've written your speech and know what you want to say, use notes or note cards to practice from, not your script. This helps you get comfortable in "speaking" to your audience, not "reciting" to them.

5. **Help Points**: Due to the nature of the exercise and speech in this lesson, **you will not be able to hold notes or cards during these activities.** If you really feel you'll need some kind of reminders or hints during your speech, here are a couple of ideas:

   a. Make a **poster board** to set aside in the room somewhere that you can see it, but is not too visible to your audience. Capture your major points in a series of bullets in <u>very large type</u> that you can see from a distance. No more than 1 to 3 words each. Or...

   b. Create a series of **3x5 cards** (or similar) with your points in logical order. Before your speech, lay them out on the floor between you and your audience where you can see them. You should have no more than 1 to 3 large words on each card.

10.4 PRESENT

It's almost time for the big show. Here are a few final notes.

1. Try to build some excitement around your event. Tell them they'll be participating (but not how) and it will be very fun.

2. If you are going to set up note card or a poster for your speech, prepare and practice with them in the place you will be giving your speech.

3. The day of the event, double-check to make sure you have everything (note cards, poster, pose ideas, action ideas, etc.).

Finally, review the **Do/Do Not Table** for a quick list of the things you'll want to do vs. the things you should avoid. Don't worry if you do some do not's or do not do some do's. Eventually it will all be second nature to you.

DO/DO NOT TABLE Lesson 6	
DO	**DO NOT**
• Smile, gesture, and have fun.	• Do not stop and restart if you make a mistake or forget. **Just keep going no matter what.**
• Use your voice and proper breathing.	
• Have a conversation with your audience.	• **Do not apologize** for making a mistake or forgetting.
• **Give the poses and actions your full effort**—make them count.	• Do not apologize about your poses or actions. **Just do them.**
• Keep going, even if you mess up.	• Do not be afraid to make a fool of yourself, your audience will love you for it.
• Be animated, cheerful, excited.	
• Have fun!	• **You do not need to be perfect.**

10.5 SPEECH TIME

It's finally time to get ready for your speech. This section will help you prepare, right up until show time. **If you're not sure exactly what to do, you should find it here.** Oh, and don't forget to video your speech event—you'll be glad you did.

10.5.1 Audience Preparation

Your audience does not have to prepare (unless you want to give them some poses and actions). The Announcer can just bring them in and give them instructions.

> NOTE: We'll assume that you've decided to give the audience a jar/cup with poses or actions that they can draw from. However, you can set this up however you like.

When it is time, bring the audience into your "auditorium" and seat them in the proper place for your speech. The audience should be given instructions similar to the following once they are seated.

ANNOUNCER

- "Welcome and thank you for attending - **Student's Name** - speech for Level 1, Lesson 6. Your participation is very important.

- We have a very exciting and fun event planned this evening and we need your to help.

- - **Student's Name** - will be out shortly and give a 2 to 3 minute speech—twice.

- While he is giving the first speech, we need you all **to reach into this jar and pull out a note with a pose**.

- **Every two sentences**, someone must **yell out a new pose** for the speaker. **Yell it loud!** Keep doing this until he's done.

- When the student is done, he will take a one minute break before giving the speech again.

- We will provide new notes. This time, you must **instruct the student to perform actions, movements, or dances**.

- Remember, someone **MUST** yell out a new **action** approximately **every two sentences. Yell loud!**

- **Your** excitement and encouragement are critical to keeping the student's momentum going.

- Now, Ladies and Gentlemen, it's time for the speech. With a round of applause, I'd like you to welcome - **Student's Name** -."

Use your imagination or embellish the introduction if you like. If there are multiple students, do the introductions for each other. If there is only one student and a small audience, you can do the instructions and introduction yourself (with appropriate adjustments) or get one of your audience members to do it. Try and make this an "event" for everyone.

10.5.2 STUDENT PREPARATION

By now, everything should be ready and you should be prepared for the exercise and speech.

- You have **practiced out loud** and know your speech well.

- You have eliminated your reliance on your notes.

- You are prepared to **give the poses and actions your all**!

- Your audience is seated and has been given instructions.

And now... it's speech time !

10.5.3   LESSON 6 EXERCISE/SPEECH

Finally, you're ready to go and it's time. This section gives you a general idea of how the event should go.

THE EXERCISE, STEP-BY-STEP!

10.5.3.1 EXERCISE – POSE ME LIKE A STATUE

1. As soon as you're introduced, step in front of your audience and **smile at them**. Remember, **don't start speaking until you are firmly in place** and have your audience's attention.

2. Start with your **arms and hands hanging loosely** by your side.

3. Begin speaking. By the time you finish the **2nd sentence** or so, someone should have shouted out a pose.

4. Immediately do an exaggerated pose, while continuing to give your speech. **Do not pause your speaking** while you move into position. Just get into position while talking.

5. When you are finished with your speech, stand straight, hang your arms loosely to your sides, and **smile at your audience**.

6. Give them a **warm thank you** and let them know you'll be back out in one minute.

ANNOUNCER

- *"Wow, that was exciting!*

- *We'll take a minute now and exchange your "pose" cards for some new "action" cards.*

- *This time, you'll do exactly the same thing, but you'll be yelling out actions, movements, or dances for the speaker to perform while speaking.*

- *Should be very interesting. Remember, yell loudly!*

- *Now, Ladies and Gentlemen, please welcome* **- Student's Name -**.*"*

10.5.3.2 SPEECH – BODY LANGUAGE BOOGIE

1. As soon as you're introduced, step back in front of your audience and **smile at them**. Remember, **don't start speaking until you are firmly in place** and have your audience's attention.

2. Start with your **arms and hands hanging loosely** by your side. Begin speaking.

3. By the time you finish the **2nd sentence** or so, someone should have shouted out an action.

4. Immediately begin doing the action, while continuing to give your speech. **Do not pause your speaking** while you start the action. Just keep moving and talking.

5. When you are finished, stand straight, hang your arms loosely to your sides, and **smile at your audience**.

Take a deep breath, relax, and hang out with your audience. They made an effort to support you and attend your speech. Spend some time with them and get feedback.

- Don't forget to give them the **Analysis and Scoring Sheet** now so that they can fill it out and provide feedback.

Last bit of advice... **relax and have fun** with all this. You're audience wants to have fun, they want you to succeed, they want to help.

So, go forth and be a proud Gabberz!

10.6 ANALYSIS & SCORING

Below is your **Analysis and Scoring Sheet** for this lesson. **Hand the sheet to your audience as soon as you have completed your speech event.**

Your **Self-Assessment Checklist** follows that. Complete that yourself as soon as the event is over while the event is still fresh in your mind.

ANALYSIS & SCORING SHEETS – LESSON 6

INSTRUCTIONS FOR AUDIENCE SCORING:

Audience Members: please work together to score the speaker in the identified categories. Please provide honest input to help the speaker identify both strong and weak skills.

AUDIENCE: Rank the following categories from 1 to 5: 1 = Needs Work/Strongly Disagree 5 = Excellent/Strongly Agree	1 to 5
The Speaker appeared prepared and confident.	
The Speaker appeared to know the speech well.	
The Speaker did not have to refer to notes very often.	
The Speaker performed two speeches—one with audience posing and the second with audience-directed actions.	
The Speaker performed the speech well in spite of being distracted by the poses and actions.	
The Speaker smiled a lot and seemed to enjoy the speech.	
The Speaker looked at and engaged the audience frequently.	
The Speaker talked clearly and loud enough for the audience to hear.	
The Speaker varied voice and tone to make the speech interesting.	
Comments:	

SELF-ASSESSMENT BY THE STUDENT:

Please rank yourself fairly to see how you improve over time.

STUDENT: Rank the following categories from 1 to 5: 1 = Needs Work/Strongly Disagree 5 = Excellent/Strongly Agree	1 to 5
Nobody threw eggs or rotten fruit at me.	
I knew my speech well and did not have to refer to notes.	
I made a real effort to do all the poses and actions to the best of my ability (and entertain my audience).	
The posing and actions did not interfere with my ability to give the speech.	
I felt prepared and ready when the time came.	
I had fun and enjoyed giving the speeches.	
I would like to do speeches like these again sometime.	
I would like to do this with a larger audience.	
I understood the directions and instructions for this lesson and had no problem completing the task.	
Comments:	

10.7 CONGRATULATIONS! PREPARE FOR LESSON 7

Congratulations on completing this lesson. We're excited about what you must be feeling by now. You are well on your way to becoming a *Gabberz Master Speaker*. Here are a few things you need to prepare.

- **FIRST!** Thank everyone for their support and let them know that you have another speech in about **3 weeks**.

- When that's done, **take a deep breath and relax**. But not too much, there's work to be done for Lesson 7.

- You'll be writing another speech for Lesson 7, but this one should be fairly easy for you.

www.gabberz.com

Gabberz Public Speaking for Kids, Tweens, and Teens
Level 1, Single-Student, Do-it-Yourself

CHAPTER 11

LESSON 7—SELF-CONFIDENCE

What You'll Learn in This Chapter:

✓ You can **choose** to be self-confident

✓ It is a skill you can learn and develop

✓ Techniques to build self-confidence

11 LESSON 7—SELF-CONFIDENCE

11.1 OVERVIEW

11.1.1 INTRODUCTION

The good news is that **confidence is a quality you can learn, develop, and grow**. No matter how *UNconfident* you might feel now, you will get better as you move forward in developing your speaking skills and gain more experience.

Confidence is <u>**not**</u> a mystical skill that some have, but others don't. There's **no magic elixir**, **no magic pill** you can take that will give you confidence. If it's not something you feel already, it **is** something you can build within yourself.

Having come this far in the program, *you should already be feeling some of that confidence growing in you*. In this chapter, we'll give you some of the tools you'll need to **help you begin to develop full self-confidence**.

Lesson 7 Overview	
Preparation Time	**3 Weeks**
Schedule	Date _____ Day _____ Time _____
Lesson	You will give one speech that you will write. Your speech should be at least 5 minutes long.
Exercise	No exercise is required for this lesson.
Speech	You will write a speech about **something you are passionate about**. You will use the tools we've given you to build your confidence.
Goals	Write and deliver a longer speech. Gain confidence in yourself.

11.1.2 CHOOSE TO BE CONFIDENT

11.1.2.1 GENERAL

Self-confidence is a marvelous trait. If we observe it in others, **we admire it** (generally). If we're <u>not</u> self-confident, **we want it**. But when we have it, **we don't think about it.**

How about you? *Do you speak with confidence?*

If not, we've got *more* great news for you. **You can "choose" to be self-confident!** In this regard, you don't have to be anything other than what <u>you</u> choose to be. Do you **want** to be self-confident?

Read on and see how you too can be self-confident.

11.1.2.2 BE POSITIVE

Your inner thoughts, or interior dialogs (talking to yourself), are important in driving what you feel and how you act. There's **NO** *metaphysical, metaphorical,* or *mystical* aspect to this. **You are simply the best person in the world at convincing *yourself* that you are good or bad at something.**

Consider the following two ways of thinking about your upcoming speech. With these thoughts running through your head, **which do you think will give you more self-confidence?**

NEGATIVE OR POSITIVE	
• I **can't** do it.	• Yes, I **know** I can do this!
• I might **fail**.	• I **WILL** succeed!
• I'm **too** nervous.	• I'm nervous, but I **can** do this!
• I'm **too** scared.	• I'm **crazy excited!**
• **What if** (<u>fill in the blank</u>)?	• This will be **good practice!**
• I might **forget** some points.	• If I forget, **I'll just keep going!**

The conversations you have in your head are like **big, giant, motivational—or <u>de</u>-motivational—magnets**. Negative thoughts like *"I'm nervous"* attract attitudes of *"I might fail"* or *"I might embarrass myself."* However, positive thoughts like *"I'm excited about doing this"* attract attitudes of *"I want to succeed"* or *"I can't wait to share my story!"*

The cool part of this? **You're doing it all in your head** and no one else will ever hear you. No one can tell you you're wrong. You can be as positive as you want—even as *outrageously* **positive** as you want—and no one will ever know about it or contradict you.

11.1.2.3   START WELL

So, how do you get started? We'll give you some tips and techniques in this lesson to help you along the way. Remember! **You don't have to memorize any of this**. We'll reinforce everything over and again thru the entire program. Eventually, it will all come to you naturally.

You've already started by **<u>thinking positively</u> and getting in the right frame of mind**. For your first tip, we'll concentrate on how to start your speech. A good, strong start goes a long way to giving you the **confidence and momentum** to keep going and finish strong.

In earlier lessons, we've stressed that you should **work extra hard on your opening lines**. The reason for this is to give you confidence when you start. *Don't undermine that hard work* by starting with an <u>excuse</u> that lowers the audience's expectations. Do **NOT** to start with:

- *"I'm really nervous, so bear with me."*

- *"Please forgive me, I didn't have time to fully prepare."*

- *"I don't know much about this topic, but I'll do my best."*

- *"I can't find my notes, so I'll wing it as best as I can."*

- *"Some of you probably know more about this than me."*

- *"I'm not the best speaker..."*

- And other negative momentum killers.

When you begin your speech, that's when you have 100% of your audience's attention. That's when you whip out your well-prepared and well-rehearsed opening lines.

Grab your audience and hold on to them.
That will give you confidence to continue strongly.

No, not like that!

11.1.2.4 TIPS TO BUILD SELF-CONFIDENCE

You could easily find thousands of suggestions in books and online on how to build self-confidence. We're going to provide a few here that are **relevant to this stage** of your training.

1. <u>Prepare</u>: **P**roper **P**rior **P**reparation makes all the difference. Spend a lot of time on preparing your material and you will be much more confident in presenting it.

2. <u>Practice</u>: What more can we say... **practice, practice, practice**. Don't delay. Don't procrastinate. Maybe practice won't make you perfect, but it will make you confident in your abilities.

3. <u>Audience</u>: Remember, **communication is about your audience**, not you. Even if your speech is about you or something you did, you are communicating it to your audience. Put yourself in their minds so that you they can engage with what you're saying.

4. <u>Passion</u>: When you have a passion or enthusiasm for what you are speaking about, your confidence builds many-fold. Your audience feeds off that passion. **Find the passion in anything you talk about**. Make it personal. Build a story from the heart.

5. <u>Fear and Nervousness</u>: We devoted earlier training to this. Turn it around and use it to give yourself energy and purpose. **Convince yourself that you are "excited"** rather than "nervous". Remember our discussions about **positive interior dialogues**?

6. <u>Tell a Story</u>: Audiences love stories! If your entire speech is not a story in itself, try to weave a "story" into it. The more personal to you and your audience, the better. Your speech should never be a list of facts—always find a way to turn those facts into a story or an analogy. **It will be easier to remember**.

You want passion? I'll show you passion!

7. <u>Eliminate "Only" and "Just"</u>: Never qualify your statements with "**only**" or "**just**". Never say, "*I am <u>only</u> a...*" or "*I <u>just</u> have...*" Be bold and declarative, "*I **am** a...*" or "*I **have**...*"

8. <u>3 to 5 Talking Points</u>: Try to distill your speech down to 3 to 5 major talking points. This makes it **easier to remember**.

9. <u>Clear Message</u>: Try to define a clear message from your speech. Don't muddy it with numerous conflicting messages.

10. <u>Self-Sabotage</u>: Sometimes, out of fear or anxiety, we may sabotage our own success (delaying preparation, excuses for not practicing, speaking too softly, etc.). Be cautious of this.

11. <u>Believe in Yourself</u>: If you don't believe in yourself, that shows. Even if it's possible that some of your audience knows more about your topic than you, they will appreciate when you get up to speak. **Believe** you are credible. **Believe** that you are **supposed** to be up there.

One last point... If you **really** want to overcome any nervousness or anxiety and **be self-confident** in your speaking (whether to one person or one thousand) **you can!** You might have to work hard at it, but you can convince yourself to be self-confident. **Your desire to be self-confident will give you the strength** to make it happen.

Choose to be self-confident!

11.1.3 GOALS

We have two main goals. We've worked on tools to help you such as **voice, body language, interaction, eye contact, preparation,** and much more. Try to incorporate a little bit from each of those lessons to make it **fun, interesting,** and **entertaining** for both you and your audience.

1. <u>Goal 1</u>: *Write and deliver a longer speech of 5 minutes.* That's part of the reason you've got 3 weeks for this lesson. Take the extra time to prepare properly and learn the material.

2. <u>Goal 2</u>: *Gain confidence in your abilities.* With a longer speech and longer preparation time, you can use what you've learned so far to prepare well. Choose to be self-confident.

11.2 PREPARE

11.2.1 WHAT YOU'LL BE DOING

This is your "**What You'll Be Doing**" table. It gives you an overview of everything that will be happening during your event. You can come back here if you get lost as to what you're supposed to be doing.

What You'll Be Doing – LESSON 7	
What	You will not be doing an exercise in this lesson. You will be giving a 5 minute speech that you must write.
When	Date _____ Day _____ Time _____
Who	Schedule your speech with **as many people as possible**. You should start to see if you can (with your parent's permission) invite others to your event (extended family, friends, etc.).
Where	Your audience will not be interacting directly with you so they can be seated anywhere facing you. Usually, about TV distance or farther is about right.
Prepare	Some preparation will be required for the speech. **Pick a speech topic you are passionate about**, then write it and practice it. **VERY IMPORTANT**: PICK YOUR TOPIC QUICKLY AND GET STARTED. DON'T DELAY!
EXERCISE — Lesson 7	
What?	No exercise is required for this lesson (or you can make one up).
SPEECH — Lesson 7	
What?	Write a speech based on something you know very well or are very passionate about. Give the speech one time to your audience (you can do it multiple times if you like).
Length?	5+ minute speech read at **normal speaking speed**. Time yourself during practice.
Special Notes	You can use props, poster boards, or whatever you like to make your speech more interesting—but don't do so much that it detracts from your personal presentation.
Subject?	Your speech can be real or fiction, a story, an event, informational, etc. You choose the topic. It can be about anything you like as long as you have a personal interest or connection to it.

11.2.2 EXERCISE

No exercise is necessary for this lesson, however, you are welcome to do one if you feel it will help you build confidence for this lesson.

11.2.3 SPEECH

COME BACK HERE AFTER YOU'VE READ THE ENTIRE CHAPTER.

11.2.3.1 SPEECH OVERVIEW

"Writing a speech is so easy, even I can do it."

It's time to start your speech. **Decide on a topic quickly** so that you can get started on writing and preparation. The result of your preparation will be at least a **5** minute speech that you will present **clearly, passionately, proudly, and confidently**. That means:

"Okay, maybe not. But it is easy."

1. You'll want to work harder at **learning the story of your speech** because you want to present this confidently, and the best way to be confident is **plenty of proper prior preparation**. Remember, you don't want to "memorize" your speech, you want to *learn* the "story" so that you can tell it in a "conversation". Being passionate about your topic will certainly help in this regard.

2. You'll have to write a longer speech than usual. This should be fairly easy though. You've had some practice writing speeches now and know what to expect. You'll also be writing about something you know well, and/or are passionate about. The words should come to you easily.

Also, while giving your speech, you'll want to use some of the connection tools we've talked about (**eye contact, movement, body language**, etc.). Not only will these techniques help **your audience engage with you**, they will help you engage with your audience so that you can have an exciting "**discussion**" with them.

11.2.3.2 WRITE YOUR SPEECH

Do not be intimidated by speech writing. Like anything else, you get better at it with practice and experience. *And what do we say about Level 1 of this program?* **You cannot do it wrong, as long as you get up and do it.**

Your speech does **not** have to be great prose. It does **not** have to be the greatest speech ever. It just has to be something that you can present with confidence and passion.

Don't worry about writing the perfect words now!

The words you need will come to you. How you present yourself will do the rest.

START EARLY AND DECIDE ON A TOPIC QUICKLY. YOU CAN ALWAYS CHANGE YOUR MIND LATER.

Let's get an idea for your speech!

1. This speech should be **5 minutes or longer**.

2. Normal speaking averages about 120 to 175 words per minute. That means you'll need to write a speech of about **600 to 900 words** or so. You'll be telling your story and the words will flow out of you when you get up on stage. **Timing your practices** will let you know if you have enough information for your speech.

3. Where to get ideas? They're all around you. Let's start with your **Scribbling/Idea Book**. Maybe there's a good adventure story. Where have you travelled? What fun things have you done? Has anything exciting, dangerous, or painful ever happened to you?

4. What **tales of adventure** do you tell your friends when you get together? Maybe there's a story you already tell that you can expand on and embellish.

5. Your tale doesn't have to be completely true. You can tell a tall tale if you like. **Your imagination has no limits**—and neither does this speech. Get wild and go for it. (*Disclose afterwards that you made it up*.)

"I always wanted to be shot into space. Then, we found this rocket and..."

6. Just remember, this should be something you are excited about, passionate about, and/or know very well.

You don't have to have the perfect idea when you start. It might change as you get into the story. **Just get <u>started</u>** gathering material. The rest will come to you as you start writing.

Let's start writing!

1. **First step**—Get out a sheet of paper or computer now!

2. **Write down your title and opening sentence at the top of your paper**. Make it something exciting. A teaser. You want to grab your audience up front and give yourself confidence for the rest of the speech.

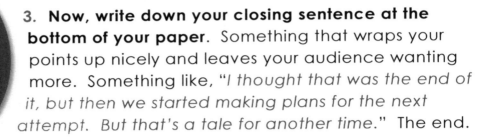

"The Doc said my eyes would be fine if I didn't do that again.

Well, I always found it hard to turn down a challenge.

The end."

3. **Now, write down your closing sentence at the bottom of your paper**. Something that wraps your points up nicely and leaves your audience wanting more. Something like, "*I thought that was the end of it, but then we started making plans for the next attempt. But that's a tale for another time.*" The end.

4. **Now, go to the middle of the paper**. Write down some **short** notes on the main action that happened between the opening and closing. **You don't need all the detail or flow at this time**, just the primary points of action, the steps, or the general sequence of events.

5. **Now, you can start filling in the white space**. What is the main point? What happened before the main point? What happened after the main point? Who was involved? How were they involved? Where were you? What did you do? What did they do? What was the result? Was it good? Bad?

6. See how easy it was to create an outline? Now that you have all the main points down, you can grab a fresh sheet of paper and **start filling in some detail for each of the points** in the outline. It should be easy to flesh out your story now.

11.3 PRACTICE

In general, you should spend greater than **80% of your time on preparation and practice**, and less than **20% on content**. If it's something you know and/or are passionate about, the content will come fairly easy. The words, phrases, voice, and presentation will come from your preparation and practice.

Practice for the Confidence Speech

This cannot be stressed enough—in order to build confidence in presenting this speech, **you need to prepare well and practice, practice, practice.** You can refer to notes or cards during your speech, but keep it to a minimum. **You want to maintain eye contact, a smile, and a connection** with your audience as much as possible.

So, here are a few tips for practicing for this speech.

1. **Writing your speech early.** The sooner you have your speech, the more time you'll have to practice it. **Don't wait until it's perfect to start practicing** (you're not reading it word-for-word anyway).

2. **Always practice out loud.** No matter where you practice, be sure to practice at the volume you think you'll need in your event room. Include movements, body language, smiling, etc.

3. **Use speech cues if you need them.** You can use a sheet of paper with just your main points on it, or 3x5 cards, or whatever you like to help you stay on track. Just make sure what you use is quick to read, easy to use, and non-distracting to your audience.

4. **Learn your story.** Remember, **you are NOT memorizing the speech** word-for-word. You are learning your "story".

"Okay, maybe I'm a little over-prepared!"

11.4 PRESENT

It's almost time for your speech event. Here are a few final notes before the big show.

1. A couple of days before your speech, verify that everyone in your audience still plans to attend.

2. If you have prepared any notes, posters, or anything else that you'll use during the speech, verify that they are ready and work as you anticipate. Do a dry run practice or two in your event location if possible.

3. The day of the event, double-check to make sure you have everything you need. You don't want to start late.

Public Speaking for Kids, Tweens, and Teens – Confidence for Life!

Finally, review the **Do/Do Not Table** for a quick list of the things you'll want to do vs. the things you should avoid. Eventually it will all be second nature to you.

DO/DO NOT TABLE Lesson 7	
DO	**DO NOT**
• **Choose** to be self-confident.	• **Do not open with an apology** or something to lower expectations.
• Step onto the "stage" with confidence.	
• **Get fully in place** and get your audience's attention before starting.	• **Do not apologize** for making a mistake or forgetting.
• **Smile** and gesture openly.	• Do not stop and restart if you make a mistake or forget. **Just keep going no matter what.**
• **Stand tall** and straight.	
• Look your audience in the eye and **talk with them**.	• **Do not fear** an audience who only wants you to succeed.
• **Keep going**, even if you mess up.	• **Do not worry** about being perfect. Just be yourself.
• Be animated, cheerful, excited.	

11.5 SPEECH TIME

11.5.1 AUDIENCE PREPARATION

Your audience has no role in this event other than to sit back and be entertained. Be sure to engage them during the event by smiling and interacting with them.

When it is time for your speech event, you or your Announcer should bring the audience into your "auditorium" and seat them in the proper place for your speech. The audience should be given instructions similar to the following once they are seated.

Announcer:

• *"Welcome, and thank you for attending* - **Student's Name** - *speech for Level 1, Lesson 7. Your participation is critical to the student's success in this training.*

- *Today, no audience participation is required, other than to sit back and enjoy the speech.*

- *- **Student's Name** - will be out shortly and give a 5 minute speech on _____.*

- *The focus of this lesson is on self-confidence. After the speech, please provide feedback on the speaker's confidence level.*

- *Now, Ladies and Gentlemen, without further delay, it's time.*

- *With a round of applause, I'd like you to welcome*
  *- **Student's Name** - ."*

Use your imagination or embellish the introduction if you like. If there are multiple students, do the introductions for each other. If there is only one student and a small audience, you can do the instructions and introduction yourself (with appropriate adjustments). Try and make this an "event" for everyone.

11.5.2 STUDENT PREPARATION

By now, everything should be ready and you should be fully prepared for your speech.

- You have spent a lot of time preparing and practicing.

- You practiced during the preparation of your speech.

- You practiced out loud **at least** 10 times after you finished writing your speech.

- You have your notes or note cards.

- Your audience is seated.

- They've been given instructions.

- The video camera is running and aimed where you'll be standing (if someone's holding it for you, they can frame you closer.

And now... it's speech time !

11.5.3   LESSON 7 EXERCISE/SPEECH

11.5.3.1 EXERCISE – SELF-CONFIDENCE

No exercise is necessary for this lesson unless you'd like to prepare one for yourself.

THE SPEECH, STEP-BY-STEP!

11.5.3.2 SPEECH – SELF-CONFIDENCE

1. When your "Announcer" introduces you, step up in front of your audience to your designated place and acknowledge them with a **smile** and **eye contact**.

2. **DO NOT begin your speech** until you are in place, comfortable, confident, and ready.

3. When you are ready:

   a. take a **proper breath**, deep in the diaphragm, and

   b. start with your **well-practiced opening lines**.

4. Remember that you are well-prepared and that your audience is there to support you. **Confidence will guide you** the rest of the way.

5. Maintain your **passion** for your topic, remember to **smile** and **engage**, then **finish strongly**.

11.6 ANALYSIS & SCORING

If you prepared and practiced properly, your confidence levels should have been very high. The **Audience Analysis and Scoring Sheet** on the next page will give you an idea of how the audience perceived your confidence. Hand the sheet to them as soon as you have completed your event.

*Most importantly, how did **YOU** feel about it?*

Your **Self-Assessment Checklist** follows the audience analysis. You should complete that as soon as the event is over. Try to be honest with yourself.

ANALYSIS & SCORING SHEETS – LESSON 7

INSTRUCTIONS FOR AUDIENCE SCORING:

Audience Members: please work together to score the speaker in the identified categories. It is important to provide honest input to help the speaker identify both strong and weak areas.

AUDIENCE: Rank the following categories from 1 to 5: 1 = Needs Work/Strongly Disagree 3 = Average/Agree 5 = Excellent/Strongly Agree	1 to 5
The Speaker delivered a speech that was at least 5 minutes long.	
In general, the speaking speed during the speech seemed normal (not too fast or too slow).	
The Speaker appeared confident at the beginning of the speech.	
The Speaker appeared to remain confident throughout the remainder of the speech.	
The Speaker seemed to know the material and be well prepared (did not *read* the speech word-for-word).	
The Speaker smiled, made eye contact, and engaged the audience throughout the speech.	
The Speaker varied voice and tone, and spoke loudly and clearly enough to be understood.	
The speech and/or the Speaker were entertaining and kept my interest throughout the speech.	
Comments:	

SELF-ASSESSMENT BY THE STUDENT:

Please rank yourself fairly to can see how you improve over time.

STUDENT: Rank the following categories from 1 to 5: 1 = Needs Work/Strongly Disagree 5 = Excellent/Strongly Agree	1 to 5
I did not collapse into a bowl of boneless mush.	
I felt self-confident during my opening lines.	
I felt self-confident throughout most of the speech.	
I felt self-confident during the closing of my speech.	
I felt more confident than I had on previous speeches.	
I felt like I was well prepared and knew my material.	
I picked a topic that I was passionate about or knew well enough to make this easier.	
I believe that I practiced enough to be confident.	
I was comfortable in front of the audience.	
I smiled and engaged with my audience.	
I understood the directions and instructions for this lesson and had no problem completing the task.	
I had fun and enjoyed giving the speeches.	
Comments:	

11.7 CONGRATULATIONS! PREPARE FOR LESSON 8

Congratulations on completing this lesson. You are gaining confidence with every lesson and are well on your way.

Here are a few things you need to do to prepare for Lesson 8.

- **FIRST!** Thank everyone for their support and let them know that you have another speech in about **2 weeks**. Let them know it will be a lot of fun and they will be participating.

- When that's done, **take a deep breath and relax.** Spend some time talking with your audience to get a better feel about how they felt about your event.

- Then begin preparation for Lesson 8. You'll need to put on a little bit of an acting cap for this one.

www.gabberz.com

Gabberz Public Speaking for Kids, Tweens, and Teens
Level 1, Single-Student, Do-it-Yourself

CHAPTER 12

LESSON 8—YOUR FACE TELLS THE TALE

SUGGESTION !

We suggest you read __all__ of Chapter 12 first, then go back to Section 12.2.2 and work through the lesson.

What You'll Learn in This Chapter:

✓ Facial expressions should match your message.

✓ Conflicting expressions confuse your audience.

✓ Proper expressions help support your message.

"Can you think of a thousand words for my face?"

12 LESSON 8—YOUR FACE TELLS THE TALE

12.1 OVERVIEW

12.1.1 INTRODUCTION

Earlier lessons showed you how body language, eye contact, and other **non-verbal cues** affect how people react to and understand what you are saying. This time, we are going to concentrate on your face—specifically, **facial expressions**.

As they say about pictures, **"your face speaks a thousand words"**. In Lesson 8, we're going to help you make sure your face is saying the same thing your words are.

Lesson 8 Overview	
Preparation Time	**2 Weeks**
Schedule	Date _____ Day _____ Time _____
Lesson	You will do an exercise with your audience and your speech will be a reading from current events.
Exercise	You and your audience will quickly come up with a list of conflicting happy/sad or good/bad events. You will then tell a story around those events using facial expressions opposite to the emotions of the events.
Speech	You will collect events from newspapers that are both happy and sad. You'll read them with conflicting facial expressions/emotions.
Goals	You will learn how much impact facial expression has on the words you speak.

12.1.2 FACIAL EXPRESSIONS

12.1.2.1 GENERAL

You've learned in earlier lessons that **correct** non-verbal cues like body language **help your listeners focus more intently** on what you are saying. Incorrect non-verbal cues confuse the audience and undermine what you are saying.

This is especially true with facial expressions. If an audience is paying attention at all, they are watching your face and **subconsciously picking up major cues** to help them understand your words.

The human face can develop over **10,000 different expressions**, but there are only **7 universally recognized emotions** we show through facial expressions:

1. Happiness

2. Sadness

3. Fear

4. Anger

5. Surprise

6. Contempt

7. Disgust

Can you guess which emotions belongs to which face? It's pretty easy isn't it? And none of them have said a single word!

Your face is a powerful tool—especially your smile.

12.1.2.2 HINTS AND TIPS

Nothing connects you and your audience together more than your facial expressions and eye contact. Unfortunately, many people lose their facial expressions entirely when they get up to speak in front of a group. **They turn to stone with their tight lips in a grim, straight line**.

Before we get into the lesson, here are a few tips to keep that from happening.

Gabberz says smiling is contagious!

Yes, but that's a little scary...

- **SMILE**: We've said this one over-and-over-and-over. Smile! People smile when they're happy. You'll also be happy to know that **a smile is one of the most contagious things in the universe**. Learn to embrace smiling throughout your day, not just when you're speaking.

- **Passion and Feeling**: Don't rely on your words to show how passionate you are. Feel the passion, the joy, the sorrow— and show it.

- **Bigger and More Expressive**: Be alive and energetic. When you have a conversation, you make small movements and gestures. When speaking to a group, you need to be bigger, more expressive, more powerful, and use extra energy. Don't let nervousness tune you down, **use that tension to power you up**.

- **Make it Match**: Make sure your facial expressions and body language match the content of your message. Feel free to frown, shake your head sadly, or even look angry if it's appropriate.

- **Eye Contact**: The eyes are the connection between speaker and listener. **Make eye contact with your audience as individuals**. If they can't make eye contact with you, they will begin to lose their connection to you and may consider you rude or disinterested.

- **Practice Faces**: Spend time in front of a mirror practicing facial expressions. Start with the **seven universally recognized emotions** we showed you, then work on some variations. Work on expressions to punctuate your words: a wry smile, an arched eyebrow, a sideways look, a grimace, etc.

- **Be Yourself**: Most importantly, **don't fake it!** Be true to yourself. Don't try to copy other people. You can learn from watching others, but you have do what is comfortable and natural for you.

12.1.3 GOALS

Your goal for this lesson is to **learn how to relax and use your face to tell-the-tale**. Your facial expressions (including eye contact) should be expressive enough to keep your audience focused on you.

As you have probably guessed, we will be twisting things up and doing this in an exaggerated way—*as well as* reversing your emotions to reinforce the goals of this lesson.

Sound like fun? Of course it does!

Hope no one smacks her on the back while she looks like that.

12.2 PREPARE

12.2.1 WHAT YOU'LL BE DOING

Now it's time for our handy-dandy "What You'll Be Doing" table.

	What You'll Be Doing – LESSON 8
What	You'll be doing an exercise with your audience and then you'll read some newspaper articles you'll prepare ahead of time.
When	Date _____ Day _____ Time _____
Who	Schedule your speech with **as many people as possible**. The exercise will require some audience input so.
Where	You will need to interact with your audience during the exercise and write down what they say, so be sure you're in a position to do that. When you get to the speaking part, you should know where to stand by now.
Prepare	Some preparation will be required for both the exercise and the speech. Details are provided in the following sections. **VERY IMPORTANT**: Prepare your materials early and be ready.
	EXERCISE — Lesson 8
What?	You'll face your audience with a sheet of paper with a line down the middle and have them give you some fake sad/bad events to list on the left and fake happy/good events to list on the right. Once you have your list, you'll take a couple of minutes to review it, then come back and give a speech based on these lists—but your facial expressions must be opposite of what you're saying. See **Section 12.2.2** below for more instruction.
Length?	2–3 minutes to gather the list, another 2–3 minutes to review, and 2+ minutes to read the speech at normal speaking speed.
	SPEECH — Lesson 8
What?	You will give a speech read from short clippings from the newspaper like a News Reporter. However, your emotions and facial expressions must be opposite of what you're reading.
Length?	3 minute speech read at normal speaking speed. Time yourself during practice.
Special Notes	1. **Be cautious about the subject matter you are using**. i.e., if you really had an Uncle John, you don't want to be smiling and laughing while you talk about how Uncle John died. 2. Be sensitive to your audience while doing both the exercise and the speech.
Subject?	Current events, politics, sports, crime, business, etc.

12.2.2 EXERCISE

COME BACK HERE TO START.

This is a fast-paced fun exercise for both you and your audience. In short, you and your audience must come up with a list of conflicting happy/good events vs. sad/bad events. You will then tell a story around those events **using facial expressions that are completely opposite** the expected emotions of the event.

Don't worry, we'll walk you through this. It's not hard.

To do this, **all you'll need is an audience and a sheet of paper with a line drawn down the middle**. (See example on next page.)

1. First, you'll ask your audience to provide you with some happy/good events (such as someone's marriage, a birth, a new puppy, etc.). These can be fake events, so let their imaginations run wild. List those down on the right side of your paper.

...and on a sad note, my little sister's puppy died this morning.

2. Second, you'll ask them to provide some **FAKE** sad/bad events (such as a building fire, a car wreck, a computer crash, etc.). Let their imaginations run wild and get some details from them.

   CAUTION: *You should try to get them to stick to **FAKE** sad/bad events. You don't want to be smiling and laughing about your Uncle Phil's funeral that was* really *held a week ago, or to happily announce your sister's puppy died.*

3. Next, you'll take the paper with the two columns out of the room for a couple of minutes and build a story around these events – alternating good, then bad, etc. The story *can be completely nonsensical and made up*. It doesn't have to be good or logical, you just have to have happy/good and bad/sad events.

4. Finally, you'll go back to your audience and give them the speech you just made up. **Here's the twist**—you MUST give the happy/good parts with a very sad face and voice (frown, shake your head, cry, etc.). When talking about the bad/sad events, you'll be very happy (smile, laugh, sing, etc.). See **CAUTION** note above.

From the example sheet above, your speech might go like this (emotion you give is shown in brackets below):

- **[Smile/Happy]** *"I heard that some movie star got run over by a tank during the filming of a movie. I guess his career ran flat."*

- **[Frown/Sad]** *"On happier news, Cousin Betty is getting married next month to her High School sweetheart. The wedding was announced yesterday."*

- **[Smile/Happy]** *"Unfortunately, the historical Grand American Hotel in town burned to the ground last night. That was where Cousin Betty's wedding reception was going to be held."*

- **[Frown/Sad]** *"Fortunately, no one was hurt during the fire."*

You don't have to have a specific number of events listed on your paper, just be sure to **get enough material that you can throw together enough events to have a speech**. It doesn't have to tie together or be coherent. It only has to be clearly happy or sad, with your expressions telling a different tale.

Be sure your audience gives you enough material to work with.

12.2.3 SPEECH

You will present this speech like a **Newscaster** reading a teleprompter. You will read about events that you have gathered from newspapers, television, etc. However, as before, **you will read them with exaggerated opposite emotions**: *happy for sad stories, sad for happy stories.*

Here is how it works:

In today's news, there were many happy or tragic events.

1. Starting now, gather some newspaper stories, write down some television reports, and/or gather news from the Internet.

2. You should gather enough news events that you can **put together a 3 minute "Newscast"** based on the headlines and a sentence or two for each event.

3. They can be any topic or theme you like, but make sure you have sufficient **happy/good** and **sad/bad** events to fill your newscast.

4. **Put together a newscast**, alternating the happy/good stories with the sad/bad stories. This works similarly to what you did in the exercise, but you have more time to develop the events.

5. If you are set up to do this, you can give this one sitting at a table or desk (as would be done in a newscast). You can read, but **you should have practice enough that you can just glance at your notes, then look at your audience** when you are speaking.

NOTE: Don't use your desk/podium as a crutch like she's doing. Remember your body language.

6. This is especially important since **you must show exaggerated opposite facial expressions for every story.** Those expressions MUST clearly show emotions opposite from what would normally be shown for that story.

CAUTION: *This caution bears repeating. Since you will be smiling or showing joy while talking about sad, bad, or tragic events,* **be careful of the topic and how your audience might react to you showing joy for a tragic event.** <u>*Do you see how powerful just your face can be?*</u> *If you are more comfortable doing so,* **you can make up a series of absurdly fake** *sad/bad events.*

12.3 PRACTICE

12.3.1 EXERCISE

No practice is required for the exercise. However, you might want to spend some time in front of the mirror working on facial expressions.

12.3.2 SPEECH

You'll want to **practice a lot** for your "Newscast" so you can look at your audience as much as possible. You can bring some notes for your speech with you, but you shouldn't be "reading" them. If you're just looking down at your notes the whole time, you're going to lose your audience.

Here are a few practice tips for you for this lesson:

1. **Get your stories together early (like NOW)** so that you have time to get your newscast together and begin practicing.

2. Prepare good, **easy-to-read notes** with headlines and key words to keep you on track.

3. TIP: **each of your stories should be like a little mini-story**, they will be easier to remember and make it easier for you to concentrate on the emotions.

4. For this lesson, **always practice using the opposite emotions and facial expressions you plan to use** when giving the speech live.

5. For this lesson, the emotions and facial expressions are **<u>much</u>** more important than the words from your speech.

12.4 PRESENT

It's almost time for your speech event. Here are a few final notes before the big show.

1. Verify that everyone who planned to come to your event still plans to be there.

2. Prepare your notes. Do a dry run or two if possible in the location you plan to hold your event.

3. If you have a very small audience, you might want to **tip them off** that they'll need to come up with some good/ bad events during the exercise. It's easy for a large group, but very small groups can sometimes have trouble coming up with things on-the-spot.

4. The day of the event, double-check to make sure you have everything you need, such as your notes.

Finally, review the **Do/Do Not Table** for a quick list of the things you'll want to do vs. the things you should avoid. Don't worry if you do some do not's or do not do some do's. Eventually it will all be second nature to you.

DO/DO NOT TABLE Lesson 8	
DO	**DO NOT**
• **Exaggerate** your emotions and facial expressions. • Use **OPPOSITE** emotions and facial expressions. • Look your audience in the eye as much as possible. • Be **loud**, **clear**, and **decisive**. • Be **animated** and **excited**. • Keep going, even if you mess up. • **Have fun**!	• Do **not** let your face show the correct emotions. • **Do not "read"** from your notes. • **Do not stop** if you make a mistake. Just keep going. • **Do not apologize** for making a mistake. • **Do not be nervous or fear** an audience who only wants you to succeed.

12.5 SPEECH TIME

These three sections are where you'll find all the details of exactly what you need to do and how to go about it. If you're not sure exactly what to do, you should find it here. Be sure to record your speech event.

12.5.1 AUDIENCE PREPARATION

When it's time for your speech, your "Announcer" will seat everyone and do an introduction similar to the following.

- "Welcome and thank you for attending - _Student's Name_ - speech for Level 1, Lesson 8. Your participation will be critical to the success of the Exercise portion of today's speech.

- For the Exercise, - _Student's Name_ - will come out and ask you to help him come up with a list of happy and sad events. It is important that you provide highly emotional events for him to use.

- And please, especially on the sad/bad events, stick to **fake** or **fictional** events. - _Student's Name_ - doesn't want to hurt anyone's feelings.

- The Speaker will then step out for a few minutes and prepare a 2 minute speech based on those events.

- As you expect from **Gabberz** by now, this will be no straight reading. - _Student's Name_ - will attempt to confuse your emotions through facial expressions and body language.

- After the Exercise reading, - _Student's Name_ - will then deliver a pre-prepared 2-3 minute newscast.

- Now, Ladies and Gentlemen, with a round of applause, I'd like you to welcome - _Student's Name_ - ."

After your "Announcer" lays the groundwork, you'll come out with your sheet of paper and a pencil and walk them through the task.

Try to get your audience excited about participating. Pressure them to provide you events rapid-fire, as quickly as they can. This keeps the excitement up and makes it more fun for everyone—like a game. If you want, you can set a timer and really put the pressure on. (Just be sure you get enough events to be able to do your exercise.)

Sad/Bad Events
(should generally be FAKE)

Happy/Good Events
(could be real or fake)

- Someone famous died in a freak accident.
- The hotel in town burned to the ground last night.
- A hurricane hit North Dakota.
- xxx
- xxx
- xxx

- Cousin Betty's wedding to her highschool sweetheart is next month.
- We got a new puppy.
- We're going on summer vacation.
- xxx
- xxx
- xxx

After you get your list, ask them to be patient for a few minutes while you step "off-stage" and prepare your exercise speech. Don't take too long.

12.5.2 STUDENT PREPARATION

By now, everything should be ready and you should be prepared for your first speech.

- You have prepared your exercise sheet and are ready to coach your audience into participating.

- You have practiced your newscast out loud at least 10 times using opposite facial expressions and body language.

- You have practiced facial expressions in the mirror.

- You have your notes in hand.

- Your audience is seated.

- The Announcer has given them instructions.

- If you are recording the event, the video camera is running.

And now... it's speech time !

12.5.3 LESSON 8 EXERCISE/SPEECH

THE EXERCISE, STEP-BY-STEP!

You're finally ready to go. As with the previous lessons, this list is your step-by-step of how the event should go. Remember, if things go differently, that's okay! This is a general guide. This is your event, so run it the way you think it should be run.

12.5.3.1 EXERCISE – GOOD? BAD? WHAT?

1. As soon as you are introduced, step in front of your audience, look them in the eyes, and smile.

2. When you are ready, begin with some instruction on what they need to do for the exercise. Tell them they'll need to provide you a list of **happy/good** and **sad/bad** events for a speech.

3. You might want to remind them to try to stick to **fake** or **fictional** sad/bad events. You *could* say something like:

   "You know these people at Gabberz never let me do things normally. I don't want to offend anyone, so for the sad/bad events, please try to stick to fake or fictional events."

4. Get your pencil and paper ready and let your audience know you'd like to do this **rapid-fire** (set a timer if you like). When you're ready, begin.

5. Keep the pressure on, prompting them for more suggestions. Point to an individual and ask for a good or bad event. Keep pushing them until you have enough.

6. When you have a sufficient list, thank your audience and let them know you'll be back in a couple of minutes.

7. Step off-stage and quickly review your list. You can number the items in the order you want to talk to them, or you can draw connector lines to related items to tell a story.

8. Remember, your speech does **NOT** have to make sense or be logical in any way. It just has to be emotional.

9. When you're ready, have your Announcer let the audience know.

10. Step back "on-stage", face your audience, look them in the eyes, and smile.

11. When you have the audience's attention, take a proper breath, and begin.

12. Work hard to exaggerate the **opposite emotions** throughout the entire speech. The conflict between the actual words and your face, voice, and body language should have them thoroughly confused.

13. When you are done, thank your audience and step "off-stage".

THE SPEECH, STEP-BY-STEP!

12.5.3.2 Speech – Face Tells the Wrong Tale

14. Have your announcer make a very short introduction. Step back out on-stage, smile, take a proper breath, and begin when you're ready.

15. Glance at your notes if you need to, then **look up at your audience.**

16. Begin with the first event. If it's a happy/good event, be very sad, frown, shake your head, maybe even cry a little. If it's a sad/bad event, smile broadly, speak brightly/happily, maybe even offer a little laugh.

17. Continue on for the rest of your newscast. **Be sure each emotion is way over-exaggerated**. Make an effort to truly confuse your audience.

18. Again, **your newscast does not have to make any sense, be logical, or even the slightest bit true**. It only needs to be emotional.

19. Use all the tools we've given you to force your face, body, and voice to the **opposite extremes** of the events you're talking about. It can be very hard to do, but the more fun you have with it, the more fun your audience will have.

20. Remember, **your audience <u>wants</u> you to succeed**. They want to have fun with you.

21. Your audience has made the effort to support you and attend your event, so you should make every effort to give them your best.

22. You do NOT have to be perfect, just give them your best effort.

Go forth. Speak clearly. **Be a proud Gabberz!**

12.6 ANALYSIS & SCORING

Congratulations! You have completed another lesson and are well on your way to becoming a *Gabberz Master Speaker*™.

We hope you had fun pouring opposite emotion into this one. Do you see now how hard it is to use opposite facial and voice expressions. **The face, voice, and body are such a big part of communication** that, when they don't match, everything seems wrong.

Now that you see how <u>not</u> to do it, **you can appreciate the importance of doing it right**.

Here is your **Analysis and Scoring Sheet** for this lesson. **Hand the sheet to your audience as soon as you have completed your speech event.**

ANALYSIS & SCORING SHEETS – LESSON 8

INSTRUCTIONS FOR AUDIENCE SCORING:

Audience Members: please work together to score the speaker in the identified categories. Please provide honest input to help the speaker identify both strong and weak skills._

AUDIENCE: Rank the following categories from 1 to 5: 1 = Needs Work/Strongly Disagree 5 = Excellent/Strongly Agree	1 to 5
The Speaker performed an exercise **and** a speech.	
The Speaker appeared prepared and ready.	
During the **exercise**, the Speaker helped push the audience to come up with the good/bad event list.	
During the **exercise**, the Speaker developed and delivered a speech based on the good/bad event list.	
During the **exercise**, the Speaker's face, voice, and body language expressed emotions opposite of what would be expected for the event being talked about.	
For the **speech** portion, the Speaker's face, voice, and body language expressed emotions opposite of what would be expected for the event being talked about.	
During the **speech**, the Speaker spent more time looking at the audience than at the notes.	
The Speaker talked clearly and loud enough for the audience to hear.	
Comments:	

SELF-ASSESSMENT BY THE STUDENT:

Please rank yourself so you can see how you improve over time.

STUDENT: Rank the following categories from 1 to 5: 1 = Needs Work/Strongly Disagree 5 = Excellent/Strongly Agree	1 to 5
My head did not explode or even vaporize a little.	
I understood the directions and instructions for this lesson and had no problem completing the task.	
I felt prepared and ready when the time came.	
I led my audience in the exercise and **pushed them** to provide me a strong list of good/bad events.	
I was able to put together a speech/newscast from the exercise list and present it to my audience.	
For the **exercise**, I presented extremely exaggerated **opposite** facial expressions and emotions.	
For the **speech**, I presented extremely exaggerated **opposite** facial expressions and emotions.	
For the speech, I knew it well enough that I spent more time looking at the audience than at my notes.	
I had fun and enjoyed giving the speeches.	
I learned how important facial expression is.	
Comments:	

12.7 CONGRATULATIONS! PREPARE FOR LESSON 9

You are well past the halfway mark in Level 1 and have learned a lot about public speaking... and about yourself. Remember, it's just like riding a bike. The more you do it, the easier and more fun it becomes.

Here are a few things you need to do to prepare for Lesson 9.

- **Take a deep breath and relax.** But not too much, there's work to be done for Lesson 9.

- We weren't kidding about that deep breath. Lesson 9 is about pacing. You'll need a deep breath as your audience puts you through your paces.

www.gabberz.com

Gabberz Public Speaking for Kids, Tweens, and Teens
Level 1, Single-Student, Do-it-Yourself

CHAPTER 13

LESSON 9—PACING

TIP !
If you ever get lost, Section 13.5.3 provides **Step-By-Step** instructions for the exercise and speech.

What You'll Learn in This Chapter:

✓ Pacing is about more than speed.

✓ We are hard-wired to react to change.

✓ Pacing involves the art of the poet and the rhythm of the musician.

13 Lesson 9—Pacing

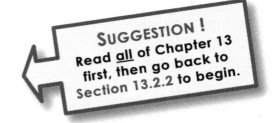

SUGGESTION !
Read all of Chapter 13
first, then go back to
Section 13.2.2 to begin.

13.1 Overview

13.1.1 Introduction

Pacing is not so much about the "speed" of your speech. The number of words per minute you speak are a part of it, but *only* a part. **Pacing as we define it is about using the tools in your speaking arsenal to keep your audience engaged and interested**. Many of the techniques you've practiced in previous lessons will naturally come into play here.

You'll learn how to use rhythm, pace, repetition, pitch, active voice, the art of the pause, and more to keep your audience engaged and interested in what you have to say. Whether speaking casually to one person, or formally to 100, **the art of pacing could make the difference** between lulling your audience to sleep and energizing them to sit up and pay attention.

Lesson 9 Overview	
Preparation Time	**2 Weeks**
Schedule	Date _____ Day _____ Time _____
Lesson	We provide a pacing speech for you in **Appendix B**.
Exercise	Your audience will direct your speed for the speech.
Speech	You will to give an impassioned Gabberz-provided speech (see **Appendix D**) using pacing tools.
Goals	Learn to use pacing tools to inspire your audience and maintain interest and attention.

13.1.2 Engaging Your Audience Through Pacing

13.1.2.1 Hard-Wired to Recognize Threats

We appear to be **hard-wired to recognize and react when things around us change**. The main purpose for this might be to allow us to identify approaching threats. For our purposes, change is how we keep our audience awake and interested.

Constancy is a hazard for the speaker. Just as we appear to be hard-wired to react to change around us, **we also appear to be hard-wired** to <u>tune out</u> the things around us that <u>don't</u> change. For example, if your family has a grandfather clock in the living room, you might have noticed the chiming when it first arrived. Very quickly though, **your mind tuned it out as a non-threatening constant**. You rarely notice it any more.

The same is true when you are speaking. You don't want to be an actual threat, but **you do want to keep your listener(s) engaged by introducing constant change into their environment**.

If you stand unmoving, speak at a constant pace, a constant tone, a constant tempo, **your listener will quickly start to lose focus and attention**. This is natural. The hard-wiring in their mind has told them that it is safe and they don't need to pay attention. So, unless they make a conscious effort to stay engaged, they will quickly slip away.

The actual words you use are, of course, important to the quality and effectiveness of a speech. However, **the true power of communication** lies in both the speaker and the listener being engaged with each other.

13.1.2.2 THE FOUR P'S

This **change vs. constancy** struggle is a critical concept for a speaker to grasp. Constancy lulls an audience, while **change creates tension and expectancy**. To help maintain an attitude of change, the speaker should embrace the **4 P's** of pacing – *Pace*, *Pause*, *Pitch*, and *Power*.

PACE

The correct pace for your speech is the one that **gets you to the end on time** and **keeps your audience engaged for the entire speech**.

When a speaker is nervous, the tendency is to speed up (maybe it's a **subconscious trick to get it over with faster**). When friends who know each other well are having a lively conversation, they might speak in **short bursts up to 400 words per minute** or more. If you were to attempt that during a speech, your audience would not be likely to understand or retain much of what you said.

The fastest articulate talker in the world has been clocked at over 650 words per minute.

Public Speaking for Kids, Tweens, and Teens – Confidence for Life!

I needed a nap anyway...

Conversely, **speaking too slowly risks your audience becoming bored and impatient** because their minds want to go faster than you are speaking. If you pay close attention to your audience and make sure you are connecting, you'll get clues to indicate if your speaking speed is too fast or too slow.

The average talking speed for a speaker is approximately **120 to 175 words per minute.** What's most important though, is to **vary the speed appropriately to the content of your message (sometimes even within a sentence) and to stay connected with your audience.**

This is where practice comes to your aid. You can time yourself so you recognize when you're rushing. It's also helpful to record yourself and listen for pacing problems.

PAUSE

The **art of the pause** and the **musical beauty of silence** have been lost for many speakers. When a group of people are talking together, you will rarely hear a pause or silence because **our natural tendency is to fill any silence with *something*.** The fear in a group conversation is that, if you pause, someone else will jump right into the silence and you'll have to try and find a way back into the conversation.

However, as the one giving a speech, you'll rarely be interrupted so **you have the luxury of using pauses and silence to achieve much greater impact.** A pause or silence can be used to:

- create anticipation or expectation;

- achieve impact or effect;

- add emphasis;

- build suspense;

- create a moment of reflection;

- give you time to remember your point.

Public Speaking for Kids, Tweens, and Teens – Confidence for Life!

Gabberz®

A pause is also great to allow your audience a moment to absorb some important or profound point you've just made.

Learn to **use the pause artfully and don't be afraid of silence**. We'll work on these during the speech portion of this lesson.

Gabberz says, "Silence is golden!"

PITCH

Just as in music, you can vary the pitch of your voice up and down the scale to create variety. *Properly* used, **pitch can "color" your voice** to provide emphasis, create excitement, and make certain words or phrases stand out.

We won't be working on pitch during this lesson, but additional lessons will help you fine tune your vocal instrument to be a master vocal musician.

For now, just try to **vary your pitch appropriately so that you are not speaking in a monotone**. Also, try to avoid any kind of repetitive pitch habits that are repeated over and over.

POWER

We haven't talked yet about volume. "Power" is about more than just volume (loudness). It is also about **modulating the intensity of your voice** (as well as your facial and body language) to create emphasis or passion.

By cranking up the intensity, the volume, and the energy at *just the right times*, **you can create a sense of excitement and anticipation** that can bring your audience to the edge of their seats, or bring them to tears.

13.1.2.3 BRINGING IT ALL TOGETHER

If you were to silently read the printed words from a great and inspiring sermon you'd heard, you *might* find the written words flat, average, possibly even rambling. But speakers who know the power of the Four P's understand how to use these tools to **create wonderful word pictures and build momentum and passion through pacing, pauses, pitches, and power**. Great orators understand that the words are important, but **connecting with and engaging the audience** is critical to delivering a memorable and effective speech.

Public Speaking for Kids, Tweens, and Teens – Confidence for Life!

Inspire yourself to inspire others.

Words on paper can be inspiring, beautiful, and memorable, but **a great speaker will bring those words to life with a powerful delivery that can stir the heart.**

Can you be that great orator?

Of course you can!

13.1.3 GOALS

Your goal for this lesson is to understand what the **4 P's** are and to try and apply these (as well as the other tools from previous lessons) to **connect** and **engage** with your audience.

The exercise will be about pace and breathing. The speech will be about using pause and power to connect with your audience.

13.2 PREPARE

13.2.1 WHAT YOU'LL BE DOING

At last, it's time to find out what you'll be doing in Lesson 9.

What You'll Be Doing – LESSON 9	
What	You'll start with an exercise with your audience (see **Section 13.5.3**), then you'll read a pre-written speech (see **Section 13.5.3**).
When	Date _____ Day _____ Time _____
Who	Schedule your speech with **as many people as possible.**
Where	Your audience will interact with you during the exercise, but not the speech. Everyone should be able to see and hear you clearly and you should stand about TV distance from your audience if possible.
Prepare	You do not need to write a speech (we have provided a great one for you in **Appendix D**), however **you should take significant time to study and practice the speech.** That's why we've given you 2 weeks for this lesson. **VERY IMPORTANT:** Pay close attention to the instructions and detail for the speech portion. You will want to make a real effort to engage your audience.

EXERCISE — Lesson 9	
What?	*The Conductor.* This is a warm-up exercise to get your vocal chords limbered up and to begin engaging your audience. Your audience will direct your speaking speed while you read the provided speech.
Length?	2 to 3 minute speech depending on how your audience directs you.
SPEECH — Lesson 9	
What?	*Famous Speech.* You will read the Gabberz-provided speech in **Appendix D**. The speech will contain special notes to help guide you in applying the 4 P's. You **must** give an impassioned speech that engages your audience.
Length?	4 to 5 minute speech read at normal speaking speed. Time yourself during practice.

COME BACK HERE AFTER YOU'VE READ THE ENTIRE CHAPTER.

13.2.2 EXERCISE—THE CONDUCTOR

The exercise is easy to prepare for, but might be a little challenging in execution. All you need to do to prepare is practice your speech. Oh, and **you'll need to find a director's baton, a spatula, a stick,** or something your audience can use to conduct your speaking speed. (You should know by now that it's never as simple as reading a speech.)

In earlier lessons, we did some work on breathing, voice, and speed. Mainly, what you'll work on during this exercise is breathing. You'll need to concentrate on breathing properly (and quickly) to **maintain a good, strong voice no matter what speed you are speaking**.

Here is what's going to happen:

1. When it's time for the exercise, you (or your assigned Announcer) will explain to your audience that you will be giving a speech and that, during the speech, a member (or members) of the audience called "**Conductors**" will use the baton/stick to control your speaking speed from extremely slow to very, very fast.

2. You must give the speech to the best of your ability while changing your pace according to the Conductor's direction.

3. The Conductor must continually change your speed up and down throughout the range of slow and fast. Their goal will be to try and trip you up, cause you to lose your place, or lose your breath. **Your goal will be to speak clearly and breathe properly** throughout the exercise.

Public Speaking for Kids, Tweens, and Teens – Confidence for Life!

NOTE: you can either assign a single person to be the Conductor for the entire exercise, let them conduct in one minute increments before passing on the baton, or let them work it out for themselves.

Faster! Faster! You must obey the Conductor!

4. The speech will contain notes and directions for pauses, pacing, and other direction. **You must <u>ignore those notes</u> during the <u>exercise</u>** and concentrate on delivering the speech at the speed indicated by your Conductor.

5. When the speech is given properly, it is 4 to 5 minutes long. Your Conductor will most likely have you talking more on the faster side than the slower, so it could take as little as 3 minutes.

So, why are we making you do this tortuous and seemingly pointless exercise? It's important for a couple of reasons. We will be doing a lot of work on proper breathing over the course of the program and this is one of the first steps. We also want to help give you a feel for what excessively fast or slow speaking feels like in a speech environment.

13.2.3 SPEECH—FAMOUS SPEECH

You have 2 weeks to practice your speech. We've prepared it for you, so spend the time wisely and get plenty of time really working on your **4P's.**

Not to be confused with the 3P's from Chapter 6:
- *Preparation*
- *Practice*
- *Presentation*

You will present this speech like a great **Orator** or **Politician.** You must know your speech well and **really try to feel the passion underneath this great speech.** In fact, you should watch several versions of this given online. Just search for "*give me liberty or give me death*" on YouTube or similar video service. There are many bad versions, but watching these will give you some idea of the power of the 4P's.

And don't forget, we're doing an abbreviated version of the speech to fit in the 5 minute window, so ours won't be exactly the same.

Surprise! There are **no** tricks or twists to this one. You're just trying to give a great speech. Here is how it works:

1. Study and practice the speech so you **know it well.** It contains some 4P instructions, but **feel free to improvise for yourself.**

2. Prepare note cards, a notes page, or a highlighted version of the speech. If you can do it from memory or simple note cards, that will help you most. But don't worry if you're not ready for that yet.

3. You should stand in front of your audience and **use your whole body to present using the 4P's.**

4. Don't exaggerate too much like we have been pushing you to do on previous lessons. You want to make this a **real, from-the-heart speech that stirs your audience** and inspires them.

5. Just stand up and give the speech to the best of your ability.

Remember: *As long as you get up and do your best,* **you cannot do it wrong in Level 1.** *Make the effort and you'll see how rewarding it is.*

13.3 PRACTICE

You'll be giving the same speech during your Exercise and your Speech portion, so the practice is pretty much the same. The only difference between the two is that, <u>during the exercise</u>, you won't be following the 4P's instructions written into the speech.

Here are some tips for practicing for this speech:

1. Remember all of your **previous practice tips** (practice often, practice out loud, etc.).

2. Make sure you **understand the 4P's** we've discussed in this section.

3. **Silence is Golden!** Whether you need a moment for yourself, or you want to pause to let your audience absorb what you've said, silence is okay. In fact, **silence can be very powerful.**

4. **Learn your speech!** You are giving this as an orator or politician, so you should not get up and just read it. Try to learn this one well so you can spend your time engaging with the audience, not "reading" the speech. (*It's okay to use the speech pages for the Exercise portion.*)

VERY IMPORTANT POINT !

5. <u>**Improvise and do it in your own style**</u> during practice. We've provided tips in the speech to apply the **4P's**. However, **these are only suggestions**. Adjust, shift, change, or *do whatever you think will make the speech more inspiring* for your audience.

6. **Remember**, this is about **YOU** connecting with your audience. You know them, we don't, so add your own flavor to the speech.

You can only accomplish tips 4 through 6 above if you practice, practice, practice. Oh, and did we mention that you should practice?

13.4 PRESENT

We're almost there. It's almost time for your big event. Here are a few final notes before the show.

1. Do a dry run or two if possible (set everything up and practice as if it were the actual event).

2. The day of the event, double-check to make sure you have everything you need (notes, baton, etc.).

Finally, review the **Do/Do Not Table**. Don't worry if you do some do not's or do not do some do's.   Eventually it will all be second nature to you.

DO/DO NOT TABLE Lesson 9	
DO	**DO NOT**
• Smile and connect. • Use pace, pause, pitch, and power. • Use the 4P's to inspire and engage your audience. • Try to sway your audience with your delivery. • Keep going no matter what. • Be loud and clear. • Be animated and ever changing. • Look your audience in the eye. • Have fun!	• **Do not apologize** for making a mistake or forgetting. • Do not stop and restart if you make a mistake or forget. **(Use a moment of silence to recover.)** • Do not be unchanging. • Do not be bland and monotone. • Do not fear exposing your passion to your audience. • Do not fill a silence **just** to fill it.

13.5 SPEECH TIME — Yaaaay!

If you're not sure exactly what to do, you should find it here. Oh, and don't forget to record your speech event.

13.5.1 AUDIENCE PREPARATION

Your audience will have a leading role in the Exercise, but not during the Speech. You should let them know this.

The audience should be given instructions similar to the following once they are seated (adjust however you like):

- *"Welcome and thank you for attending - Student's Name - speech for Level 1, Lesson 9. Your participation is critical.*

- *We have **2 activities** today. You will have a major role in the first.*

- *[Hold up the wand or stick.] During the exercise, **you** will have the power to make the speaker talk faster or slower at your slightest whim. Sound like fun?*

- *Throughout the exercise, whoever holds the speed wand must raise it like this to (speak really fast now)make-the-speaker-talk-much-faster,-or-lower it like this to (speak really slow now) to... make... the... speaker... talk.... real..... slow.....*

- *[Talk normal now.] Be sure to change the speed a lot to make it interesting. You can even wave it up and down to make it challenging. Try to trip up the speaker if you can. You can choose among yourselves who will have this **amazing** power. [Hand the wand to them.]*

- *The second activity is a famous speech the student will deliver.*

- *The speech has been modified in order to keep within our program time limits.*

- *Your only role during the speech will be to sit back, enjoy, and then provide feedback when the event is over.*

- *Now, Ladies and Gentlemen, it's time to begin. With a round of applause, I'd like you to welcome - Student's Name ."*

Use your imagination or embellish the introduction if you like. If there are multiple students, do the introductions for each other. If there is only one student and a small audience, you can do the introduction yourself (with appropriate adjustments). Try and make this an "event" for everyone.

13.5.2 STUDENT PREPARATION

By now, everything should be ready and you should be prepared for your first speech.

- You have practiced out loud **at least** 10 times.

- You have your speech notes in hand.

- Your audience is seated.

- They've been given instructions.

- The video camera is running.

THE EXERCISE, STEP-BY-STEP!

And now... it's speech time !

HAVE FUN!

13.5.3 LESSON 9 EXERCISE/SPEECH

You'll start with the exercise, then deliver your speech.

Exercise – The Conductor

1. As soon as you are introduced, step in front of your audience, look them in the eyes, and smile.

2. When you are ready, remind them what they need to do for the exercise. **Tell the Conductors they are free to do their best to try and trip you up.**

3. When you're ready, take a good breath from the diaphragm, tell your audience you're ready to begin, and ask the Conductor to hold the wand in the center.

4. Ready? Start!

5. Start speaking at normal speed. **You can ignore most of the 4P's and the instructions for the exercise.** Just concentrate on breathing and speed as directed by the Conductor.

6. Watch the wand closely and try to **immediately** change speed according to the Wand's position.

7. Adjust your speed from **very, very, excruciatingly slow** (when the wand is low) to **very, very, absurdly fast** (when the wand is high) The faster or slower you can do it for your audience, the more fun they (and you) will have.

8. Watch your breath and, no matter what the speed is, speak in a **full voice** and <u>**enunciate clearly**</u>. Enunciation is very important.

9. When you are done, smile at the audience and thank the Conductor(s).

10. Let the audience know that you'll take a very short break to catch your breath and will be right out to deliver your speech without the speed wand.

THE SPEECH, STEP-BY-STEP!

Speech – Famous Speech

11. When you are ready, have your announcer make a **very short** introduction.

12. Step back out on-stage, smile, take a proper breath, and begin.

13. Glance at your notes when you need to, then **look up at your audience**. Keep your connection with them.

14. Use all the tools we've given you to **incorporate the 4P's** to engage your audience.

15. Remember that, if **you** don't care, your audience won't care. Use your own passion to draw them in and deliver a speech that will inspire and engage them.

16. Really reach down deep inside and have fun with it. Your audience wants you to succeed.

17. Remember, you do NOT have to be perfect, you just have to be yourself and give them your best effort.

Go forth. Speak clearly. **Be a proud Gabberz!**

13.6 ANALYSIS & SCORING

Here are your **Analysis and Scoring Sheets. Hand the sheet to your audience as soon as you have completed your speech event.** Your **Self-Assessment Checklist** follows that. You should complete that yourself as soon as the event is over.

ANALYSIS & SCORING SHEETS – LESSON 9

INSTRUCTIONS FOR AUDIENCE SCORING:

Audience Members: please work together to score the speaker in the identified categories. Provide honest input to help the speaker identify both strong and weak skills.

AUDIENCE: Rank the following categories from 1 to 5: 1 = Needs Work/Strongly Disagree 5 = Excellent/Strongly Agree	1 to 5
Exercise	
The Speaker did an exercise with the speed of the speech varying from slow to fast, led by a Conductor.	
During the exercise, the Speaker was understandable and clear while speaking both very slow **and** very fast.	
Speech	
The Speaker delivered a famous speech with passion.	
I felt engaged and inspired by the speech.	
The Speaker kept my attention by varying speed, pitch, and position.	
The Speaker used pauses, emotion, and expression to vary the delivery and keep my interest.	
The Speaker appeared to believe what he/she was saying.	
The Speaker appeared prepared and did *much more* than just read the speech.	
Comments:	

SELF-ASSESSMENT BY THE STUDENT:

Please rank yourself fairly to see how you improve over time.

STUDENT: Rank the following categories from 1 to 5: 1 = Needs Work/Strongly Disagree 5 = Excellent/Strongly Agree	1 to 5
The audience did not shove me in a box and try to sell me off as a circus oddity.	
I understood the directions and instructions for this lesson and had no problem completing the task.	
I was prepared and ready for the exercise/speech.	
I had fun with the exercise and did my best to go really fast or really slow.	
I had practiced sufficiently that I was comfortable giving the speech and engaging my audience.	
I used the 4P's throughout my speech to engage the audience and try and inspire them.	
I learned that a good speech is about more than just words.	
I am beginning to feel excited about the prospect of giving more speeches.	
I think the audience had a good time and I'm glad I did this.	
Comments:	

13.7 CONGRATULATIONS! PREPARE FOR LESSON 10

Congratulations on completing this lesson. I'm sure you did a great job and you're well on your way to becoming a *Gabberz Master Speaker*.

Here are a few things you need to do to prepare for Lesson 10.

- When that's done, **take a deep breath and relax**. But not too much, there's work to be done for Lesson 10.

- For Lesson 10, we plan to have a little fun with your audience, so be sure to get as many people as you can to attend.

www.gabberz.com

Gabberz Public Speaking for Kids, Tweens, and Teens
Level 1, Single-Student, Do-it-Yourself

CHAPTER 14

LESSON 10—HAVING FUN

TIP !
Section 14.5.3 provides Step-By-Step instructions for the Exercise and Speech.

What You'll Learn in This Chapter:

✓ Public speaking is fun.

✓ Humor can be very powerful, but risky.

✓ You don't have to tell jokes to have fun with your audience.

Public Speaking for Kids, Tweens, and Teens – Confidence for Life!

Gabberz®

14 LESSON 10—HAVING FUN

14.1 OVERVIEW

14.1.1 INTRODUCTION

SUGGESTION !
Read __all__ of Chapter 14 first, then go back to Section 14.2.2 to begin the lesson.

We stress the need to "**connect**" with your audience. **Rarely** will your audience ever want a statue-like figure standing on stage <u>reading</u> to them. *Yawwwwn...* There's no faster way to put an audience to sleep.

In **Lesson 10**, we'll bring a few things together and have a little fun with the audience. You'll try to **build a deeper bond** through one of the primary human connectors... humor.

Don't worry, even if **you** don't think you're funny, you (and your audience) will have fun here. **Trust in yourself.**

Lesson 10 Overview	
Preparation Time	**2 Weeks**
Schedule	Date _____ Day _____ Time _____
Lesson	You'll use some of the tools you've learned to connect with your audience through humor.
Exercise	You and the audience will write a short speech together.
Speech	You will write a speech based entirely on rhetorical questions.
Goals	You will learn that humor (and not necessarily jokes) help a speaker connect with an audience.

14.1.2 EVERYONE WANTS TO BE ENTERTAINED

Consider the following formula:

Didn't know this would involve math...

> Your audience *wants* **you** to succeed

> **+** <u>Your audience *wants* to be entertained</u>

> **=** Your audience **wants you to succeed** at entertaining them

Treat your audience as a partner in your adventure and they will happily join in with you to provide the momentum you need to truly connect.

We're going to jump in pretty quickly to the exercise and speech, but there are a few things to cover first. To make the most out of this lesson, you'll want to dust off some of the tools and techniques you've learned so far.

- Look your audience in the **eye** and **smile** at them.

- Smiles are particularly important for this lesson. You'll be amazed at how far a **good, wry or knowing grin** can go in life.

- **Be bold. Be confident. Be positive** in your inner dialogue.

- Use the **4P's** to the max. Pace, pause, pitch, and power all need to be a part of your speaking arsenal. The **Dramatic Pause** will be especially important in the speech portion of upcoming lessons.

- "**Read**" your audience to see what's working and what's not. Learn to recognize what entertains them.

14.1.3 GOALS

The goal for this lesson is simple. It is to relax, let yourself go, and **have some fun**. In the process of that, your audience will have some fun too.

14.2 PREPARE

14.2.1 WHAT YOU'LL BE DOING

What You'll Be Doing – LESSON 10	
What	You will be doing an exercise with the audience and then delivering a speech based on rhetorical questions that you have written.
When	Date _____ Day _____ Time _____
Who	Make this fun and **get as large an audience as you can**. The more, the merrier. Ask your attendees if they know anyone else they'd like to invite. *Maybe you can offer cookies as an incentive.*
Where	During the exercise, your audience will need to work together to come up with a list of made-up words. They should interact with each other with someone writing down their results. For the speech, you'll want to be able to move around. You don't have to be able to get close to *everyone*, but you should be able to interact in general.
Prepare	Some preparation will be required for this lesson. The exercise will only require you to prepare a sheet of paper for your audience. However, you will need to write and practice a speech. **VERY IMPORTANT**: This speech is a little different. Get started early to allow yourself plenty of time to write it, refine it, and practice it.
EXERCISE — Lesson 10	
What?	Your audience will create a list of nonsense words under your direction that you will then use to improvise a short speech. More detail is provided in **Section 14.2.2**.
Length?	2 to 3 minute speech using **only** the words provided by your audience.

Public Speaking for Kids, Tweens, and Teens – Confidence for Life!

Gabberz

SPEECH — Lesson 10	
What?	You will write and deliver a speech that is made up entirely of rhetorical questions. You must deliver the speech in a **fast-paced** drive that hammers your audience with questions while using dramatic pause and the 4P's for effect. Details are provided in **Section 14.2.3**.
Length?	3 to 4 minute speech read at normal speaking speed. Time yourself during practice.
Subject?	You will choose the subject. The speech can actually be completely random with numerous topics and subjects.

COME BACK HERE **AFTER** YOU'VE **READ** THE ENTIRE CHAPTER.

14.2.2 EXERCISE—THE BABBLER

Although there is very little preparation needed for this exercise, it will challenge your skills quite a bit. Not only will you need to give this "speech" with **all the super powers of your 4P's**, you'll need to **improvise your speech in a couple of short minutes** from a series of nonsense words your audience will provide for you.

Doesn't that sound like a good bit of fun?

It is, if you're willing to embrace the exercise and just relax and let yourself go with it. Remember the formula from before? The audience wants to have fun, and **they want you to be successful at having fun with them**.

Here's how it all works:

1. Prior to the event, you will prepare a sheet of paper with 3 boxes at the top and some space to write below (see example to the right).

2. You will need to instruct your audience that they are to come up with **15 completely nonsense words**. The funnier the words, the better. They should provide 5 words with one syllable, 5 words with two syllables, and 5 words of three or more syllables.

3. Give the audience as much time as they need to come up with words they really like. Be sure they are providing **fun nonsense words**.

Example Only

5 – One Syllable Words	5 – Two Syllable Words	5 – Three or More Syllable Words
Ooog	Marklar	Skigledo
Skib	Budbe	Mishtofu
Bood	Zarful	Youpino-ino
Rall	Hoopug	Nomashtifibi
Zuf	Studle	Cantugorg

Speech:

No problem! I speak nonsense all the time.

4. When they are done, thank them and let them know you'll need 4 or 5 minutes to prepare.

5. Now, go off somewhere and prepare yourself to **give a speech using only these 15 nonsense words.** Use the space on the sheet to either write a couple of sample sentences, or write the words in larger, clearer letters to use as a cheat sheet during your speech.

6. Take the rest of the time you have (if any) and say the words over-and-over to get more familiar with them.

As I'm sure you're expecting by now, here's the Gabberz Twist...

7. You must use these 15 words and all your learned skills to try and inspire your audience with an impassioned speech. You can't just spout out a 3-minute jumble of words. **Your voice, face, and body language must give color and meaning to the words.** And make your audience believe.

8. How do you do that? You start with the 4P's, throw in some heavy eye contact, and just a dash of acting.

9. Here are a few things you can do to add belief to your speech:

   a. Make use of **Dramatic Pauses.** We'll talk more about dramatic pauses throughout the program.

   b. **Act it out.** Pretend you're doing something so that it is assumed the words are related to the actions.

   c. Fake **dramatic questions** and try to get your audience to **nod yes or shake their heads no** with you.

   d. **Pull one of the audience members on stage** with you and point out their clothing, hair, hands, shoes, or whatever comes to mind. It doesn't have to mean anything. It just adds a visual element that gives life to the words.

   e. Do anything that adds a **visual** or **motion** queue to give the words a fake life. (You really should video this exercise.)

10. MOST OF ALL... **be animated, be bold, be forceful, and really hammer home the words like you mean them.**

11. So, using only the words you've been given, your speech might go something like...

   "Zarful. Ooog marklar skigledo? Budbe Skigledo? [shake your head and point to someone] *Cantugorg rall zuff rall bood. Rall bood? Nomashtifibi budbe skib ooog.* [raise your voice with passion] *Skib ooog nomashtifibi! Ooog mishtofu, ooog cantugorg! Ooog cantugorg zuf zarful.* [dramatic pause, lean in towards audience and growl] *Studle ooog nomashtifibi. Nomashtifibi !!!* [shake your head like they've missed the point] *Marklar budbe marklar. Skib budbe studle. Skigledo!* [bow and say] *Zarful !"*

Obviously, the words make absolutely no sense. Your mission is to make your audience **believe** your speech has some meaning. You must use all the tools at your disposal to accomplish this. Now is the time to **uncork your inner-ham and lay out some real acting**.

Why does this work at all? You may remember the **3V's Rule** from an earlier lesson:

3V's Rule

According to some studies, an audience's perception, comprehension, and feelings are gathered from these 3 factors:

   VISUAL = **55%** (body language, appearance, etc.)

   VOCAL = **38%** (tone, timbre, inflection)

   VERBAL = **7%** (the actual words that were said)

See how it's all starting to come together? Give this one some real effort and have fun with it. Your audience will be glad you did. *You might even want to turn it into a party game.*

14.2.3 SPEECH—THE RHETORICAL QUESTIONATOR

You will hear advice from time-to-time that you can warm up your audience by starting out with a joke. You may tell some jokes in later lessons, **but jokes can be risky if not delivered right, and to the correct audience.** We highly recommend that you get significant speaking experience and learn to read your audience and improvise before resorting to joke telling.

Instead, as you've seen throughout this program, there are other ways to engage and have fun with your audience. You've just seen that in the exercise. **If you have fun with it, your audience will too**.

We're going to go a different way with your speech so that you can use the other tools in your speaking toolbox to engage and entertain your audience. This is similar to the question-asking speech you gave in an earlier lesson but, this time, you'll be asking the questions.

This time, you will write a speech that consists entirely of "Rhetorical Questions" that you will rapid-fire at your audience.

> **Rhetorical Question defined**: *"A statement that is formulated as a question but that is not supposed to be answered. Asked simply to make an assertion or produce a dramatic effect, but <u>not</u> to elicit a reply."* Some examples:

- *"Who knows?"* (Implies that nobody knows.)

- *"You don't expect me to go along with that crazy idea, do you?"* (Implies express disagreement.)

- *"Can you please quiet down?"* (Implies a command.)

- *"What business is it of yours?"* (Implies that it is not your business and you should mind your own.)

- *"Is the sky blue?"* or *"Does a bear live in the woods?"* (Implies something is obvious or correct.)

- *"Why are you so stupid?"* (Implies, um, duhhhh...)

Gabberz Twist

Why couldn't we leave well enough alone? (*A rhetorical question.*) You know we have to twist things up a bit. For your speech, you are welcome to use rhetorical questions as defined above, but we think you and your audience will have a whole lot more fun if you use the **Gabberz Twisted Definition**.

> **Gabberz Rhetorical Question defined**: *"A nonsensical question that has no real answer. Asked simply to confuse and confound. Any attempted reply could only be just as nonsensical."* Some examples:

- *"If a tree falls in the forest, who does the squirrel sue?"*

- *"If that's the best thing **since** sliced bread, what was the best thing **before** sliced bread?"*

- "If practice makes perfect, and no one's perfect, then why make sliced bread in the first place?"

- "If pigs flew and birds tasted like bacon, what would we eat for breakfast?

Technically, nonsensical questions are not considered **proper** rhetorical questions. *But, when have we ever been considered proper?* (You don't have to answer... that was a rhetorical question.)

An entire speech made of proper rhetorical questions would get boring pretty quick. That's why **we want you to use the Gabberz Twisted Definition** and make it as interesting and fun as you can. **Just let your imagination run wild**.

You'll use the **4P's** (particularly your Power Voice) and your passion to move your audience to try and answer your questions—even though they don't really have answers. You'll use Pace and Pause to suck them into **quickly responding with *the first absurd thing that pops into their minds***. Make it move fast and keep them engaged.

Here's how The Rhetorical Questionator works:

1. First, you need to write a 3 to 4 minute speech based entirely on series of nonsensical Gabberz-twisted rhetorical questions.

2. The topic can be anything you like **or** nothing at all. You'll probably want to go free-range and use numerous topics as thoughts occur to you. The weirder and harder to answer the questions are, the better.

3. One of the hardest things you'll find is that **it's tough to use the 4P's in a short question format like this**. You'll need to put all your new super powers to use on this one.

4. On some questions, you might want to do a **short lead-up** to your question to give yourself time to use some of the 4P's. Maybe something like, "*Even in the protection of a forest, trees are subject to aging, drought, fires, floods, and more. So, the real question that occurs to me is... if a tree falls in the forest, and no one's around to hear it, who does the squirrel sue?*" With a lead-in like that, you have some time to really lay on the 4P's.

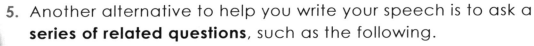

> **What if nothing pops into my head?**

5. Another alternative to help you write your speech is to ask a **series of related questions,** such as the following.

- *"Considering the technological and other wonders of today's world, is sliced bread **really** the best we can come up with to compare things to?"* [Audience answer.]

- *"If something new is the best thing **since** sliced bread, what was the best thing **before** sliced bread?"* [Audience answer.]

- *"Which makes me wonder... if practice makes perfect, and no one's perfect, then **why** make sliced bread in the first place?"* [Audience answer.]

6. You must get an answer (or non-answer) from your audience on every one of your rhetorical questions.

> **In Level 1, you cannot do the lesson wrong. Just get up and do something.**
>
> **Of course, everyone will have more fun if you really put your heart into doing the lesson as designed.**

7. When your audience is gathered, you or your Announcer will **give them instructions to answer the questions as quickly as they can with** <u>the first absurd thing</u> **that pops into their minds—no matter how nonsensical.** You can either have them free-for-all to answer, or raise their hands to be picked by you. You decide which will create the most excitement.

Remember, you are responsible for reading your audience and keeping things moving at a brisk pace. **Keep moving, keep your pace up, use your power voice to command attention.** Most of all, make your audience respond to you by answering your questions.

14.3 PRACTICE

Probably the hardest thing will be using the 4P's effectively. Since you are doing this in short chunks (your questions), it will be a challenge to use pace, pause, pitch, and power to move your audience to respond.

But you can do it! This is where diligent practice comes in. Get your questions created early so you have time to practice this format.

Practice enough that you can use short notes or a cheat sheet for the queues you need to keep this moving quickly. Here's how you **practice.**

1. Start out using your full questions written out clearly on a sheet of paper. **Read them "<u>to</u>" something** (a pet, a plant, a mirror, etc.) so that you begin pulling your eyes from the sheet to connect.

2. As you read, start building in some of the 4P's. Take notes on where you think you should pause, pick up the pace, exaggerate inflection, raise your voice, or use other verbal tools.

3. Once you think you've got a decent grasp on that, start with your question #1 and **practice that one by itself** 10 or 15 times, really pushing hard on the 4P's.

4. Then move to your 2nd question, and so on. Don't skimp. Spend serious time learning each question, pushing harder each time.

5. Now, **create some abbreviated notes or cards** and start practicing from those. You can use them if needed during your speech event, but you shouldn't have to rely on them.

6. When you practice, really put yourself in your audience's place and try to do what you think would move them to respond to you.

Put some effort into practice so you can concentrate on your audience. You don't have to remember the questions word-for-word. Just give yourself some short-short notes to remind you what you're supposed to be asking, and the question will come to you easy enough of you've practiced sufficiently.

For this lesson, **it will probably help to spend most of your practice time working on each question individually**, rather than working on the speech as a whole. That way, you can work in detail on the 4P's for each question.

14.4 PRESENT

It's almost time for your speech event. Here are a few final notes before the big show.

1. Make sure your exercise sheet and notes or cards are ready. Do a dry run or two if possible in the same place for your speech.

2. The day of the event, double-check to make sure you have everything you need.

Finally, review the **Do/Do Not Table** for a quick list of the things you'll want to do vs. the things you should avoid.

DO/DO NOT TABLE Lesson 10	
DO	**DO NOT**
• Smile and gesture.	• Do not be shy about being silly.
• Encourage your audience to participate.	• Do not stop and restart if you make a mistake or forget. **Just keep going no matter what.**
• Force yourself to do 4P's when giving your questions.	
• Engage with your audience and help them share the experience with you.	• **Do not apologize** for making a mistake or forgetting.
• Look your audience in the eye.	• Do not just toss a question out there. Give it all you've got... and then some. Demand an answer.
• Keep going, even if you mess up.	
• Be animated, cheerful, excited.	• Do not be bland and monotone.
• Be loud and clear.	• Do not fear an audience who only wants you to succeed.
• Let the force of your voice demand answers, even nonsensical ones.	
• Have fun!	• You do not need to be perfect.

14.5 SPEECH TIME

These four sections are where you'll find all the details of exactly what you need to do and how to go about it **step-by-step**.

14.5.1 AUDIENCE PREPARATION

Your audience has a role in both the exercise and the speech and should be given instructions similar to the following.

- *"Welcome and thank you for attending - __Student's Name__ - speech for Level 1, Lesson 10. Your participation will be extremely helpful to the student's completion of the **Gabberz Public Speaking Program**.*

- *There are two events today. The first is a short exercise, and the second is a question and answer session.*

- *During the exercise, - __Student's Name__ - will have you fill out a sheet of paper with 15 complete nonsense words of 1, 2, and 3 or more syllables. **The sillier, more nonsense they are, the better.** But they cannot be real words.*

- *Once you provide those 15 words, the student will take 4 or 5 minutes to prepare, then will come back and **give a 2 minute speech using ONLY those words**.*

- *Following that, the student will return for the speech portion.*

- *However, instead of a regular speech, <u>- Student's Name -</u> will ask you a series of rhetorical questions that have **no real answer**.*

- *Your job as the audience will be to answer all questions as quickly as you can, keeping the momentum going.*

- *You do **not** need a correct answer because **there is <u>no</u> correct answer** to any of the questions. **Any** answer will do. But <u>you must answer as quickly and nonsensically as you can</u>. **Yell out the first absurd thing that comes to your mind.***

- *When the session is done, you will do the regular survey questions.*

- *Now, Ladies and Gentlemen, it is time. With a round of applause, I'd like you to welcome <u>- **Student's Name** </u>.*

Use your imagination or embellish the introduction if you like. Try and make this an "event" for everyone.

14.5.2 STUDENT PREPARATION

By now, everything should be ready and you should be prepared for your first speech.

- You have practiced out loud numerous times.

- You have your exercise sheet and speech in hand.

- Your audience is seated and has been given instructions.

- The video camera is running. **We highly recommend that you record this event!**

- Do some proper breathing and tell yourself you're going out there to have some fun.

And now... it's speech time !

14.5.3 LESSON 10 EXERCISE/SPEECH

14.5.3.1 EXERCISE – THE BABBLER

THE EXERCISE, STEP-BY-STEP!

1. As soon as you're introduced, step in front of your audience, look them in the eyes, and give them a big, warm smile.

2. Hold up the word sheet you've prepared and remind them what they need to do.

   "*As we said in the introduction, you need to provide me with **15 made-up nonsense words**. I'll take those, and make a speech out of it.*"

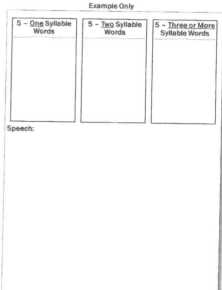

Example Only

5 – <u>One</u> Syllable Words	5 – <u>Two</u> Syllable Words	5 – <u>Three or More</u> Syllable Words

Speech:

3. Give them whatever instructions you like, but keep pushing to come up with the silliest, most nonsense words they can.

4. When they finish the list, tell your audience to relax for 4 or 5 minutes while you prepare.

5. Leave the room and write out the words larger or prepare some sample sentences to use to start you out. Then practice the words with what time you have left. **Don't leave your audience sitting too long.** They will get bored. *Maybe they can watch your old speech videos to see how you've progressed.*

6. When you're ready, have your Announcer introduce you. Walk up and **give them a big, cheesy smile,** then begin.

*It does **NOT** matter if you mess up all the words. As long as they're nonsense, that's all you need.*

7. **Don't be shy. Ham it up.** Really **convince** your audience you are trying to say something real. **Make the words come alive!**

8. When you are finished, have your Announcer let the audience know you will now move into the speech portion of the event.

14.5.3.2 SPEECH – THE RHETORICAL QUESTIONATOR

THE SPEECH, STEP-BY-STEP!

9. After the short introduction, step back out onto "stage". Take a proper breath, smile broadly, and launch off with your first question.

10. Make eye contact and prompt your audience to answer the question. If no one answers right up, push them to answer. **Remind them there is no right answer, but you will need an answer of some kind as FAST as possible.**

11. The second you get an answer, launch off quickly with your second question. Maybe even interrupt them to keep up the pace and anxious anticipation.

12. Ask your questions **rapid-fire**, pushing for answers from everyone.

13. Keep the **momentum** going by keeping everyone engaged. Try to get them in the habit of fighting over who gets to answer.

14. Remember to **use the 4P's** as much as possible. Inflection and pace are especially important.

15. **When the last question is answered**, smile and thank your audience.

Your audience made the effort to support you and attend your speech. **Try to have fun and give them your best effort!**

14.6 ANALYSIS & SCORING

Can you believe it? **You've completed 10 speech events, many with multiple speeches involved.** You've already given more speeches than most people do in their entire lives. You've done things in front of an audience that you'd probably never imagined you'd do before you started with Gabberz. **And you've had a bunch of fun along the way.**

Are you starting to see now how it all ties together? All the weird little things you've had to do that might not have made too much sense in the beginning? We told you up front that all the concepts would build on top of each other, improving your skill set with each successfully completed lesson.

There's still a ways to go before achieving **Gabberz Master Speaker** status, but you've built up quite a speaking toolset already and have some real experience under your belt.

Don't forget to get your audience to do your **Analysis and Scoring Sheet** for this lesson. **Hand the sheet to your audience as soon as you have completed your speech event.**

Your **Self-Assessment Checklist** follows that. You should complete that yourself as soon as the event is over while the event is still fresh in your mind. Try to be honest with yourself.

ANALYSIS & SCORING SHEETS – LESSON 10

INSTRUCTIONS FOR AUDIENCE SCORING:

Audience Members: please work together to score the speaker in the identified categories. Please provide honest input to help the speaker identify both strong and weak skills.

AUDIENCE: Rank the following categories from 1 to 5: 1 = Needs Work/Strongly Disagree 3 = Average/Agree 5 = Excellent/Strongly Agree	1 to 5
Exercise	
We understood the instructions and the Speaker prompted us to provide 15 nonsense words for the exercise.	
The Speaker gave a speech using only the words we provided on the exercise sheet (or close approximations of those).	
The Speaker attempted to make us understand and feel engaged in the nonsense speech.	
Speech	
The Speaker gave a speech using only rhetorical or nonsense questions.	
The Speaker engaged the audience and pushed for answers to all of the questions.	
The speaker made eye contact, changed pace, changed inflection, and kept up audience interest.	
The Speaker was confident and spoke clearly and at appropriate volume throughout the speech event.	
The Speaker appeared prepared for the event.	
Comments:	

Public Speaking for Kids, Tweens, and Teens – Confidence for Life!

SELF-ASSESSMENT BY THE STUDENT:

Please rank yourself fairly so that you can see how you improve over time.

STUDENT: Rank the following categories from 1 to 5: 1 = Needs Work/Strongly Disagree 5 = Excellent/Strongly Agree	1 to 5
My internal organs did not melt down from the heat of everyone's eyes staring at me.	
The exercise with the nonsense words was fun and I'd like to do it again sometime.	
I was comfortable giving my audience direction and prompting them to fill out the word sheet.	
I was prepared for the speech (rhetorical questions) and had no trouble remembering the questions.	
I was able to "read" the audience and change my pace to keep them interested and engaged.	
I understood the directions and instructions for this lesson and had no problem completing the task.	
I believe the audience had a good time.	
I was comfortable pushing the audience to give me answers to the nonsense rhetorical questions.	
This rhetorical question format speech was fun!	
Comments:	

14.7 CONGRATULATIONS! PREPARE FOR LESSON 11

Congratulations on completing this lesson. I'm sure you are building confidence and speaking skills and are well on your way to becoming a *Gabberz Master Speaker*.

Here are a few things you need to do to prepare for Lesson 11.

- **FIRST!** Thank everyone for their support and let them know that you have another speech in about **2 weeks**.

- When that's done, **take a deep breath and relax**. But not too much, there's work to be done for Lesson 11.

- The next lesson will involve an exercise with the audience and a speech you'll need to write, so, it's time to get started.

Go forth. Speak clearly. Be a proud Gabberz!

www.gabberz.com

Gabberz Public Speaking for Kids, Tweens, and Teens
Level 1, Single-Student, Do-it-Yourself

CHAPTER 15

LESSON 11—OWNING THE STAGE

What You'll Learn in This Chapter:

✓ How to use the "stage" to enforce your message.

✓ How to move "purposefully" rather than randomly.

✓ How to project "confidence."

15 LESSON 11—OWNING THE STAGE

15.1 OVERVIEW

15.1.1 INTRODUCTION

SUGGESTION!
Read <u>all</u> of Chapter 15, then go back to Section 15.2.2 to start the lesson.

Speakers use many different types of visual aids to help their audience understand the content of their speech. They use props, PowerPoint slides, pictures, and more—frequently forgetting the most important visual aid of all... **themselves**!

You, the **Speaker**, should always be the primary visual aid that your audience focuses on. **All else is a distraction**.

In Lesson 11, you're going to begin to learn how to "**Own the Stage**" and put forth a **confident and commanding presence** that captivates and engages your audience. That's a tall order, but we'll get started.

Lesson 11 Overview	
Preparation Time	**2 Weeks**
Schedule	Date _____ Day _____ Time _____
Lesson	You will do an exercise with the help of your audience and you will give an action-based speech.
Exercise	Your audience will direct your actions and your presentation based on those actions.
Speech	You will write and deliver an action-based speech.
Goals	You will learn to use the stage, move purposefully, and project confidence.

15.1.2 IT'S YOUR STAGE—OWN IT!

From the moment you are introduced, you are on stage. **<u>It is yours and you own it</u>**. All of it!

What do we mean by that? We mean that **the entire time you are on stage, your audience's attention should be on you** and what you are saying. That's why you've worked so hard on your presence, body language, eye contact, etc.

Watch good speakers in action and you'll see that, even when they use visual aids, **they quickly draw your attention back to themselves**. This is because they understand that **the connection between the speaker and the audience is what's most important**—<u>not</u> the aids or visuals.

Too many speakers (*because they don't know better or because they're trying to hide their nervousness*) plant themselves behind a podium and try to keep the audience focused on their slides.

Now, if you'll direct ALL of your attention over there to my helpful but boring PowerPoint slides, we can get started...

The audience may get some good technical notes out of a slide deck, but **the opportunity to really connect with the audience and help them "understand" is lost**. Slides should play only a supporting role and can be given as a handout afterwards. <u>**Stage time is your time!**</u>

What Do You Mean By "Owning the Stage?"

Good question. The short answer is to use all the tools you've learned to **engage your audience so they don't want to take their eyes off of you**.

Rooaarrr!

So, how do you do that? We'll give you a few tips and tricks here (in no particular order) then build on them.

1. **ENGAGE!** From the first second, walk "on-stage" with confidence and give your audience a big, openhearted smile. Make them feel welcome in "your home" (i.e., your stage).

2. **Don't Waste Your Stage Time**: Make sure everything is set up and ready beforehand so that your audience isn't sitting and waiting while you adjust things. Be ready!

3. **Don't Pace**: Random or repetitive pacing is distracting and a sign of nervousness. **Don't pace back-and-forth like a caged tiger.** You want to move around during your speech, but it should be purposeful and deliberate.

4. **Purposeful Movement**: You own the stage, so use all of it if you like. But be sure to do it **deliberately, not randomly**. Move closer to the audience to emphasize a point or add importance. Move as you make a transition in your speech from one point to another. Move to different areas of the "stage" to focus on different groups in the audience so that everyone feels included.

5. **The 4P's**: Use the 4P's (*pace*, *pause*, *pitch*, and *power*) to firmly engage your audience and take command. Throw in some passion and you've got a real recipe for owning the stage.

6. **Keep it Simple**: Visuals, props, and other things should be simple and error free. The focus should be on you and what you have to say, <u>not</u> your stuff.

7. **Idle Hands**: Hands are troublesome things and improperly "*handled*," can be a sign of nervousness or insecurity. Many people are self-conscious about their hands and usually just jam them in their pockets or clasp them together. It's hard for most people to let them hang naturally by their sides. We'll spend time on this later. For now, just avoid fidgeting, clenching, crossing, pocket stuffing, twisting, twirling, or any other distracting repetitive behavior. However...

8. **Gesturing**: We encourage you to use your hands to make gestures to emphasize points. Well-timed and meaningful gestures to enhance your speech can be very powerful. You'll be using your hands plenty in Lesson 11 and in later lessons.

9. **Fiddling**: And speaking of hands, don't fiddle with things. Fiddling with keys, pocket change, your pen, jewelry, or anything else quickly becomes distracting. You want to appear confident, in command, and in charge—so don't fiddle (unless, of course, you are actually playing the violin).

10. **Energy and Enthusiasm**: Energy and enthusiasm is contagious. If you are bouncing with energy and beaming with enthusiasm, your audience will feel that and share in it. Go Team!

11. **Believe in Yourself**: How can you expect your audience to believe in you if you don't believe in yourself? Trust in your abilities and, if you don't feel it yet, fake it.

15.1.3 GOALS

The following exercise and speech will help you become comfortable moving around the "stage" with purpose. Your personal goal should be to project confidence—whether you feel it or not.

15.2 PREPARE

15.2.1 WHAT YOU'LL BE DOING

Don't forget about your handy "What You'll Be Doing" table.

What You'll Be Doing – LESSON 11	
What	You will do an exercise at the direction of your audience, then you will give an action-based speech you have written.
When	Date _____ Day _____ Time _____
Who	The more people you can get in your audience, the more fun everyone will have. Extended family and good friends will appreciate being invited to your event.
Where	Your audience will be calling out actions to you during the exercise. For both the exercise and the speech, you will need plenty of room to move around. Be sure your "stage" is big enough for you to demonstrate your actions.
Prepare	For the exercise, you can prepare a list of ideas for your audience, but that is not required. You will need to write a speech. **VERY IMPORTANT**: Prepare sufficiently and have confidence in your ability to do this. More importantly, try to have fun with it. You make the choice whether you see this as a burden or as something fun to do. Personally, we always choose fun.
EXERCISE — Lesson 11	
What?	You'll have to think fast on this one. Your audience will call out things involving action every 10 seconds. You must act out the action, using the whole stage, and tell the audience what you're doing.
Length?	Approximately 2 minutes.
SPEECH — Lesson 11	
What?	You must write an action-based speech that involves movement for the entire speech.
Length?	3 to 4 minute speech read at normal speaking speed.
Special notes?	You'll want to practice sufficiently so that you can give the speech without notes (**hint**: your topic of choice will be important).
Subject?	Your speech can be about anything you like, as long as the entire speech is about an action (or multiple actions) that you can act out as you're speaking. You'll want to pick a topic you are familiar with since it will be hard for you to hold onto notes (don't worry, we'll give you some tips to do this without notes in hand).

Public Speaking for Kids, Tweens, and Teens – Confidence for Life!

15.2.2 EXERCISE—THE AUDIENCE ACTIONATOR

There's not much you can do to prepare for this exercise but put on your thinking cap and decide to have fun. Your audience will be in the driver's seat and it will be up to you to make the most of it.

You will have no prepared speech for the exercise, but you will need to speak. In short, **your audience will call out "actions"** that can be physically performed and you must act out the action while telling the audience what you are doing step-by-step <u>or</u> telling a story about it.

Here's how the Exercise works:

1. <u>Optional</u>: Prior to the event, you can put together a list of actions as examples for your audience. They can choose from the list, or come up with their own. Actions can be anything with movement, but might include:

Put out a fire.	Ride a bike.	Play an air guitar.
Climb a tree.	Fight a bear.	Leap hurdles.
Vacuum the floor.	Box a <u>tall</u> guy.	Box a <u>short</u> guy.
Fly an RC plane.	Fly a real plane.	Land a plane.
Drive a race car.	Crash a car.	Have a sword fight.

   Give your audience your list, or you can just give them some examples and let them come up with their own.

2. When your audience is assembled, you will instruct them that they must yell out actions for you to perform every 10 seconds or so for the full 2-minute exercise.

3. Be sure they give you a new action **at least every 10 seconds.** Don't let your audience go too slow. They can either yell actions out randomly/chaotically, or they can take turns. Leave that to them.

4. As soon as an action is called out, **you must immediately begin** to pantomime the action. Be sure to overact and exaggerate the action. You must try to use the entire "stage" while performing the action. Move around, spread out, use all of the stage.

   "...and then I made the plane roll over twice before landing it."

Get ready, here's the *Gabberz Twist...*

5. While physically doing the action, you must either:

    a. **Describe the action** you are doing, "*I'm climbing the ladder truck 3 stories, now I'm fanning a steady stream of water into the top of the building,*" **OR**

    b. **Tell a made-up story** about what you're doing, "*When I was riding my bike once, I jumped it off an overpass onto the top of a big tractor-trailer.*" The more outlandish, the better.

6. Use all the tools you've been learning to engage your audience and make them believe. Hard to do in 10-second chunks, but that's what makes it so much fun.

7. Set a timer for 2 minutes (or have someone time you). If everyone's having fun, you can extend the time, *or even offer for some of your audience members to come up and give it a try.*

8. Remember... **be animated, be bold, be fun**!

15.2.3 SPEECH—THE ACTIONATOR

This is similar to the action speech you did earlier, but your focus will be different this time. You will not focus just on moving, but you'll concentrate on **moving around purposefully** and using the entire stage.

The end result will be a **3** to **4** minute speech with you using the stage and acting out your action the entire time. That means a few things:

- You'll want to **write a speech about something you're very familiar with.** Some activity you've done, some sport, an event you went to, a game you play, etc.

- You'll have to learn the story of your speech well because you'll be moving and gesturing the entire time. Remember, you don't want to "memorize" your speech, you want to **learn your "story" so that you can "tell" it to your audience**. We'll give you some tips to keep you on track during your speech.

- You can tell a story about something that actually happened to you, or you can make something up. Or a mix of the two. Just make it full of action and adventure.

Let's talk about your speech a little:

1. This will be a **3 to 4 minute speech**.

2. At normal speaking speeds, you'll need a speech of about **350 to 600 words** or so. There should be plenty of action and, if you are excited about the story, the words will flow out of you when you get up on stage.

   > Decide on a topic quickly. You can always change your mind later.

3. Where to get ideas? They're all around you. Where have you been? What have you done? Has anything exciting, dangerous, or painful every happened to you? Maybe there's a good action scene on a TV show or in a movie you'd like to reenact? It doesn't have to be original, it just has to be **full of action and movement**.

4. Or you could just let your imagination run wild and make up some big adventure. It's up to you.

You have a story, now what?

5. You are telling a story through both your words and actions. You'll use the whole stage and your whole body to convey detail and engage the audience.

6. Don't be distracted by your own movement and be sure to use the **4P's** to connect with the audience.

7. Use your hands expressively to show the action/activity.

8. Walk, run, jump, kneel, kick, whatever conveys the action.

9. Us the whole "stage" as your playground. Always keep moving, but try to make it purposeful and a part of the described action, not just senseless pacing.

10. Be absurd and have fun with it!

When I did an "Ollie" like this, my skateboard flew out and went through the windshield of my Dad's car.

Hopefully, you've now got an **exciting action story** loaded with plenty of opportunity for movement and over-acting. You should also be eager to share that story with your audience. **You'll see how much easier it is to remember and tell your story when <u>you</u> are excited and interested.** This excitement also helps the audience connect with you.

15.3 PRACTICE

No practice is needed for the <u>exercise</u>. Just put on your thinking and acting hats and give the audience your best. There is NO wrong way.

Practice for "The Actionator" Speech

You'll want to practice quite a bit for your speech since it will be hard to look at any notes while you're doing the action.

Here are some tips for practicing for this speech.

> **Start early and choose an action topic you are very familiar with. You'll be glad you did!**

1. **Start writing early.** The sooner you have your speech, the more time you'll have to practice. Don't wait till it's perfect.

2. **Choose a well-known topic.** Picking an action/event that you know well will help you remember the flow during your speech. A topic that has a logical flow such as a step-by-step process will also make it easier.

3. **Always practice out loud at full volume!** You'll also want to **practice the movements and actions** you're going to perform. This will help you relate the words to the action and make it easier to remember where you are.

4. **Big words and cheat sheets.** You should NOT hold a copy of your speech in your hands—*you should be using your hands*. However, you can write out **10 or so key words** on a sheet of paper and lay it on the floor somewhere nearby. You could also do a small poster and hang it facing away from your audience so only you see it. Be creative. But learn to **pick the right few words** to key you in on where you are in your speech.

5. **Learn the story of your speech.** Remember, **you should rarely ever "memorize" a speech** word-for-word. You are learning your "story" so you can "tell" it to your audience. **Just as if you were telling a scary story around the campfire.**

Public Speaking for Kids, Tweens, and Teens – Confidence for Life!

15.4 PRESENT

It's almost time for your speech event. Here are a few final notes before the big show.

1. Verify everyone in your audience still plans to attend.

2. Do a dry run or two on your "stage" if possible.

3. The day of the event, double-check everything.

Finally, review the **Do/Do Not Table** for this lesson.

DO/DO NOT TABLE Lesson 11	
DO	**DO NOT**
• Smile and gesture grandly.	• Do not stop and restart if you make a mistake or forget. **Just keep going no matter what.**
• Keep moving something—your hands, your feet, and/or your body.	
• If you "mess up," keep going, keep moving, don't stop until the end.	• **Do not apologize** for making a mistake or forgetting.
• **Be animated, grand, exaggerated.**	• Do not talk without moving something.
• Be loud and clear no matter what you are doing physically.	• Do not fear an audience who only wants you to succeed.
• Have fun!	• Nobody expects you to be perfect.

15.5 SPEECH TIME

Remember, if you're not sure exactly what to do, you can always come to this section for step-by-step instructions. Don't forget to record your event.

15.5.1 AUDIENCE PREPARATION

Your audience will have a major roll during the **Audience Actionator Exercise**, but not for **The Actionator Speech**. Let them know this up front so they can be prepared.

When it is time for your speech event, your Announcer should bring the audience into your "auditorium" and seat them in the proper place for your speech. **The audience should be given instructions** similar to the following.

BE SURE TO DO AN INTRODUCTION.

- *"Welcome and thank you for attending - Student's Name - speech for Lesson 11. Your participation is important for this one.*

- *There are 2 parts to today's event.*

- *The first part will be an exercise where you will direct the student's actions. For this 2-minute exercise, you must yell out actions such as, "put out a fire," or "ride a bike" **every 10 seconds**.*

- *The student must immediately perform the action while either describing what he's doing or telling a related story.*

- *The student has prepared a list of possible actions, but you are free to call out any action you can think of. You do not have to pick from this list.*

- *Keep it moving fast and be sure to provide a new action **every 10 seconds or less**. You are the Directors. The student is your willing puppet.*

- *The second part today is an action-based speech the student has written. The audience does not have a role except to sit back and enjoy the show.*

- *At the end of - Student's Name - speech, you will be asked to complete a short survey about today's event.*

- *Now, Ladies and Gentlemen, it's time for the exercise and speech. A round of applause please for - Student's Name - ."*

Use your imagination or change the introduction if you like. Make it exciting! It helps to have someone else do the introduction to make this an "event" for everyone.

15.5.2 STUDENT PREPARATION

By now, everything should be ready and you should be prepared for your first speech.

- You have practiced out loud **at least** 10 times.

- For this speech, we recommend that you practice more so that the speech comes more naturally to you, **like a campfire story**.

- You have a list of actions written down for the audience if desired.

- If needed, you have prepared a cheat sheet or poster with a few key words placed where you can see it easily.

- Your audience has been seated and given instructions.

- The video camera is running to capture this incredibly fun event. You should probably have someone holding the camera rather than having it on a tripod. You will be moving around so much, the camera will miss much of it.

And now... ACTION !

15.5.3   LESSON 11 EXERCISE/SPEECH

The following two sections provide a step-by-step look at what should happen for the exercise and speech events.

THE EXERCISE, STEP-BY-STEP!

15.5.3.1   EXERCISE – THE AUDIENCE ACTIONATOR

1. When you are introduced, step up in front of your audience and give them a **big smile**.

2. Offer a quick reminder of what you'll be doing for the exercise. Hand them the list of actions if you have one.

3. Ask for any questions about the exercise and see if they need time to come up with some actions. Make sure they have pencil and paper, then give them time if they'd like it.

4. When all is ready, take a deep breath and tell the audience they can begin at any time.

5. Start your 2 minutes. As soon as someone calls out an action— **begin!**

6. Start to pantomime the action, using as much of the stage as you can. Either describe the actions or make up a quick story involving the action. It can be completely false, made-up, and/or ludicrous.

7. Keep the audience on pace for new actions **every 10 seconds or faster**. Keep things fast and manic.

8. At 2 minutes, throw your hands up in the air, take a deep breath, and thank the audience for a good exercise.

9. At this point, you can also *ask if anyone in the audience would like to try.* Let as many people try as you like.

10. Tell the audience you'll be back in a moment and step off stage to catch your breath.

THE SPEECH, STEP-BY-STEP!

15.5.3.2 SPEECH – THE ACTIONATOR—STUDENT

11. Your "Announcer" should step up and say a few words to introduce you for the speech portion. He might say something like, *"Ladies and Gentlemen, a round of applause for our next speaker, _____Student's Name_____."*

12. As soon as you're introduced, step up to your spot again and smile at the audience, making eye contact.

13. Start right out with **lots of action, movement, and pantomime** of the action described by your story.

14. Try to use all of your "stage," making **purposeful movements**. It helps to time the movements so major moves emphasize changes in the story.

15. Be elaborate with your movements. Be broad. Over-pantomime while keeping your focus on the audience. Be sure you are maintaining your connection with them.

16. Make an effort to entertain your audience with a fun speech. **Get excited, use your actions as a tool** to move and motivate your audience.

17. **Try to have fun with it**. Your audience does not expect perfection. They will not judge you or make fun of you. **They want to have fun WITH you**.

18. Your audience has made the effort to support you and attend your speech. **Give them your best effort**!

Go forth. Speak clearly. **Be a proud Gabberz!**

15.6 ANALYSIS & SCORING

Hand the Analysis and Scoring Sheet to your audience as soon as you have completed your speech event. When they have completed that, you should complete your **Self-Assessment Checklist**.

ANALYSIS & SCORING SHEETS – LESSON 11

INSTRUCTIONS FOR AUDIENCE SCORING:

Audience Members: please work together to score the speaker in the identified categories. Please provide honest input to help the speaker identify both strong and weak skills.

AUDIENCE: Rank the following categories from 1 to 5: 1 = Needs Work/Strongly Disagree 5 = Excellent/Strongly Agree	1 to 5
Exercise	
The Speaker and the Announcer gave clear instructions on what was going to happen.	
The Speaker performed a series of actions directed by the audience and provided narrative with the actions.	
The Speaker made a real effort to follow audience direction and used most of the stage for the actions.	
Speech	
The Speaker told an action story describing some event or activity.	
During the speech, the Speaker was animated, moving around the "stage" to demonstrate the action.	
The Speaker appeared prepared and knew the story well enough to tell it while acting it out.	
I felt engaged with the Speaker and enjoyed hearing and seeing the activities of the story.	
I had a good time and enjoyed myself.	
Comments:	

Public Speaking for Kids, Tweens, and Teens – Confidence for Life!

SELF-ASSESSMENT BY THE STUDENT:

Rank yourself fairly so that you can see how you improve over time.

STUDENT: Rank the following categories from 1 to 5: 1 = Needs Work/Strongly Disagree 5 = Excellent/Strongly Agree	1 to 5
I did not spontaneously ignite in flames.	
I was comfortable moving around the "stage" and performing actions while speaking.	
I really enjoyed the exercise and trying to come up with actions and stories so quickly.	
I felt engaged with the audience the entire time.	
I understood the directions and instructions for this lesson and had no problem completing the tasks.	
I felt prepared and that I had practiced enough.	
I had fun doing the speech with the actions and movements to complement what I was saying.	
I felt better prepared and less nervous this time than on previous speeches.	
I am beginning to enjoy giving speeches.	
I would like find more opportunities to give speeches.	
Comments:	

15.7 CONGRATULATIONS! PREPARE FOR LESSON 12

Congratulations on completing this lesson. Here are a few things you need to do to prepare for Lesson 12, *the final lesson in Level 1.*

- **FIRST!** Thank everyone for their support and let them know that you have another speech in about **3 weeks.**

- **Take a deep breath and relax.** But not too much, there's work to be done for Lesson 12.

- **Lesson 12 is the final lesson in Level 1** and it's where you will try to bring together all that you've learned. Whether you feel it or not, **you have learned a lot**.

Good luck and happy speaking!

www.gabberz.com

Gabberz Public Speaking for Kids, Tweens, and Teens
Level 1, Single-Student, Do-it-Yourself

CHAPTER 16

LESSON 12—TIE IT ALL TOGETHER

SUGGESTION !

We suggest you read **all** of Chapter 16 first, then go back to Section 16.2.2 and begin working through the lesson.

What You'll Learn in This Chapter:

✓ How to use all your new skills to give a regular speech (no tricks this time, we promise).

16 LESSON 12—TIE IT ALL TOGETHER

16.1 OVERVIEW

16.1.1 INTRODUCTION

Awsome Job!

Congratulations, you've nearly completed Level 1 of the program.

Great job!

You've done a lot of strange and unusual things to get here (*sorry about that*). And you may have been embarrassed, nervous, and/or unsure from time-to-time. By now **you should be feeling some of the joy and excitement that comes from being a confident communicator**.

In this final lesson of **Level 1**, we're going to pull it all together and have you give a longer speech using the tools you've learned to engage and truly communicate with your audience. *No tricks, no twists… just you and your audience.*

This will be your **Level 1 Graduation Speech** if you would like to receive information on **Level 2**, register your program on the Gabberz mailing list at www.Gabberz.com.

Here's the Overview Table for this lesson.

Lesson 12 Overview	
Preparation Time	3 Weeks
Schedule	Date _____ Day _____ Time _____
Lesson	No exercise is required, only a speech the student must write.
Speech	Student must write a **6-minute** speech.
Goals	Tie all of your new skills together to give a longer speech that engages your audience.

16.1.2 GIVING A REAL SPEECH

Review

You have accomplished a lot in just 11 lessons. To refresh your memory before we get started, let's do a quick review.

Wow! Look at all the stuff you did. That's amazing!

Lesson	Title	What You Learned
Intro	**Introductory Speech**	You learned how to get an audience together and get up and read a speech in front of them.
1	**Know Fear = No Fear**	You learned that there is **nothing to fear** in giving a speech and that emotion and passion add impact to your words.
2	**The 3 P's**	You learned how to **Prepare**, **Practice**, and **Present**. You also learned some basics about writing speeches.
3	**You'll Put Your Eye Out!**	You learned how important it is to make **eye contact** and how to do it comfortably.
4	**Ummm Cruncher**	You learned about **verbal fillers** like "ummm", "like", and "you know", and how to reduce your reliance on them.
5	**Voice Control**	You learned how to **breathe properly**, **project your voice**, and speak with **confidence** and **conviction**.
6	**Body Language**	You learned how important **body language** is and some basics on how to stand, move, and use your hands. You also learned about the **3 V's rule** on comprehension.
7	**Self-Confidence**	You learned that **you can "choose" to be self-confident** and that it is a skill you can learn and develop.
8	**Face Tells the Tale**	You learned that conflicting expressions confuse your audience and **how to use facial expression** to support your message.
9	**Pacing**	You learned about the **4 P's**: Pace, Pause, Pitch, and Power, and how these are used to engage your audience.
10	**Having Fun**	You learned a little bit about **humor** (the good and the bad) and how to have fun with your audience.
11	**Owning the Stage**	You learned how to use your "**stage**" to enforce your message, **to move purposefully**, and to **project confidence**.
12	**Tie It All Together**	You'll learn how to pull all you've learned together to give a **compelling** and **engaging** speech.

Wow! That *is* a lot of stuff. But it was all necessary to provide you a solid foundation to build on as you develop more and more skills in speaking, communicating, and leadership.

Remember, **you don't have to memorize all this stuff**, we'll reinforce it all as we go along. As long as you did your best to follow instructions, you picked up what you needed.

However, there are a few rules that might get confused together that are worth a quick review.

Lesson	Rule	What Is It?
Lesson 2	**3 P's**	There are three phases of your speech. All are important: 1. <u>P</u>repare, 2. <u>P</u>ractice, 3. <u>P</u>resent.
Lesson 6	**3 V's**	An audience's perception, comprehension, and feelings from a speech are gathered from these 3 factors: 1. <u>V</u>isual = 55%, 2. <u>V</u>ocal = 38%, 3. <u>V</u>erbal = 7%.
Lesson 9	**4 P's**	The 4 P's of pacing are necessary to engage an audience: 1. <u>P</u>ace, 2. <u>P</u>ause, 3. <u>P</u>itch, 4. <u>P</u>ower.

16.1.3 GOALS

Your goal for this lesson is simple. It is to pull together all the skills and tools you've learned throughout Level 1 to give a regular speech.

This means you'll want to **reach into your toolbox and use what you've learned** to connect to your audience, engage with them, and give a compelling speech. No twists this time.

Public Speaking for Kids, Tweens, and Teens – Confidence for Life!

16.2 PREPARE

16.2.1 WHAT YOU'LL BE DOING

Here's the overview of what you're doing for your last lesson in Level 1.

What You'll Be Doing – LESSON 12	
What	You will be writing and delivering a speech.
When	Date _____ Day _____ Time _____ You should have scheduled this speech event for about **3 weeks** after you start this lesson.
Who	Throughout Level 1, we've tried to get you to expand your audience when you could, but **it is very important that you try to get a larger audience** for your Graduation Speech. Have your family reach out and see if you can grow your audience for this important event. Possibly it could coincide with another family event? Maybe a gathering at the house like the Super Bowl? (But NOT during the game.) Although the audience will not have a role (other than as the audience), **you want your Graduation Speech to be a big event** and staged appropriately.
Where	Up to this point, you've probably been doing your events in the living room or family room. To turn this into more of an "event", try to pick a larger area, set up a "stage", arrange seating, etc. None of that is required, but the more you can make this like a real speech, the better it will be as your "graduation event."
Prepare	You will need to write and practice your speech. The only preparation is to set up your event as described above.
EXERCISE — Lesson 12	
What?	No exercise is required for Lesson 12.
SPEECH — Lesson 12	
What?	You will write a speech using any subject or method you like.
Length?	6-minute speech read at normal speaking speed.
Subject?	The subject or topic of your speech is up to you. It can be about anything you like, but you might like to use some of the techniques we've given you in Level 1 to come up with a topic you can really enjoy. We'll provide some suggestions and tips in the next section.

16.2.2 EXERCISE

No exercise is required for Lesson 12.

16.2.3 SPEECH

16.2.3.1 GRADUATION SPEECH!

Okay, you've worked hard and finally made it to your last speech in Level 1. This is where it all comes together and you get to show off your **shiny new Speaking Super Powers**!

No tricks, no twists, no odd little things to do (*unless, of course, you want to do any of that stuff yourself*). Your **Graduation Speech** is a speech where you get up in front of your audience and use your skills to engage your audience, connect, and share your story with them.

16.2.3.2 PICK A TOPIC FOR YOUR SPEECH

Speaking of stories... what in the world are you going to speak about?

We leave the subject of your speech to you, but here are a few tips. Ultimately though, <u>you</u> pick what you want to talk about.

I don't need to leap tall buildings, I have the power of SPEECH!

- **Pick something you know:** Pick a topic you know well and enjoy talking about. This will make it easier to engage with your audience and remember the pieces of your speech.

- **Tell a story or describe an event**: If it's a story (real or imagined) that has a beginning, middle, and end, it will be easier for you to get into it and follow the flow of events.

- **Social or news topic**: If there's something in current events that you're really interested in or passionate about, those make great speeches.

- **Hobbies or things you enjoy**: If you have a hobby or something else that you enjoy doing, it's easy to write about it and be animated in your discussion of it. Just be careful not to bore your audience with details. Keep it animated and fun.

- **Scribbling book/Idea book**: Did you keep a Scribbling book or Idea book? You should have some great topics to choose from. Maybe you have a journal or diary? Ideas are all around you.

- **Your Gabberz experience**: We like this one of course. You could do a speech reviewing all the things you had to do in Level 1 to get to this point. You could talk about the embarrassing moments, things that went wrong, things that went right, how you felt about doing different parts, and so on. There would be lot of material there.

Whatever you choose, here is the most important tip: <u>**start early and choose a topic quickly**</u>. The worst thing you can do is wait around, trying to decide on the "perfect" topic for your speech. The sooner you can pick your topic, the more time you'll have for writing and practicing.

Pick a topic now so you can start thinking about it!

16.2.3.3 THE EVENT

Let's talk about your Graduation Speech Event now. We'd like to stress again how **you should make every effort to get a larger audience for this speech**. As your speaking prowess grows, you'll want to find larger and larger audiences to speak to. Now's a good time to start.

If you just can't get more people for this event, that's okay. **The larger audience is for your benefit.**

Here are some notes on your Graduation Speech Event:

- You will be writing and delivering a **6-minute speech**, so you'll want to use some of the speech-writing tips we gave you in Lesson 2. If it makes sense for you, you might even use one of your previous speeches as a kicking-off point. You'll need to freshen it up and expand on it if you choose this path.

- Try to make this an "event" for you and for your audience. Spend a little extra time on preparation, setting up your "auditorium" and "stage", and consider some props or maybe even treats (cookies, pastries, etc.) for your audience.

- Normal speaking speeds run around 120 to 175 words per minute, so you'll need a speech of about 700 to 1000 words. This will vary depending on the type of speech you are delivering, your plans for pacing, pausing, etc. (Note that this page is about 250 words.)

- Refresh yourself on the tools you've used up to this point. Use the 4P's and other methods to keep your speech moving briskly, maintain connection to your audience, and keep them engaged.

- Have a **strong and interesting opening** that you know very well. Come out strong and keep up the energy.

- Have a **powerful ending that wraps up your speech** and makes it clear to the audience that you are done.

- Keep everything else in the middle exciting and audience-centric.

16.3 PRACTICE

If I "read" my speech, I won't have to look the audience in their eyes.

Although you will be able to use speech notes, note cards, or whatever you like on this one, the less you rely on that support, the more you can connect with your audience. **So practice... a lot.** That's why we've given you 3 weeks on this one.

- Get the first draft of your speech done quickly so you can start practicing. Fine-tune the speech as you practice and hear yourself saying the words out loud.

- Remember, we don't write and speak in the same way. Write your speech however you like, but speak naturally and from the heart. Don't read the script.

- DON'T MEMORIZE. If you're going to memorize your speech word-for-word, you might as well read it. **You want to be real, fluid, talking with your audience**—not at them. Your speech should be like *telling a story around the campfire, under the stars*, to a bunch of friends. You don't read from notes for that. Learn your *story* instead.

- Practice out loud at the same volume you will use at your speech. You need to hear it and feel it to practice properly.

16.4 PRESENT

It's almost time for your big Graduation Speech Event. Here are a few final notes before the big show.

1. Verify that all of your attendees still plan to come. Note that it's never too late to try and find more people for your audience.

2. Do a dry run or two if possible with any props you'll use. Set everything up and practice as if it were the actual event.

3. The day of the event, double-check to make sure you have everything you need. A copy of the speech or notes, video camera, treats for the audience, etc.

Finally, review the **Do/Do Not Table** for a few reminders.

DO/DO NOT TABLE Lesson 12	
DO	**DO NOT**
• **Welcome your audience as they arrive** and help them get seated. • Let them know you appreciate them coming to support you. • When you come on stage, give the audience a big smile. • Stand tall and straight. • Look your audience in the eye and connect with them. • Keep going, even if you mess up. • Be animated, cheerful, excited. • **Decide to be confident!** • Enjoy yourself and have fun!	• Do not ignore your audience. • Do not stop and restart if you make a mistake or forget. **Just keep going no matter what.** • **Do not apologize** for making a mistake or forgetting. • **Do not lock-up trying to remember where you are, just pick a spot you know and keep going.** • You do not need to be perfect, you just need to be your best. • Do not convince yourself that you will fail.

16.5 SPEECH TIME

Are you excited? It's finally time for your Graduation Speech for Level 1. We've suggested you video all of your speeches, but we highly recommend it for this one. This is your first, big, serious speech and you'll want a record of it. And don't forget, **you can send any of your recorded lesson speeches to us for a professional evaluation (fees apply).** Visit www.gabberz.com for details.

16.5.1 AUDIENCE PREPARATION

Seat your audience in your auditorium. Make this a formal and exciting "event." Give your audience instructions similar to the following.

- "Welcome and thank you for attending *- Student's Name -* speech.

- This is the final **Graduation Speech** for level 1 of Gabberz.

- Your participation is greatly appreciated and has been critical to the Student's work towards **Gabberz Master Speaker.**

- You have no role today, sit back and enjoy the speech.

- *- Student's Name -* will be giving a 6-minute speech on _____.

- With a round of applause, please welcome *- Student's Name -*."

Make this an "event" for everyone. **Embellish, put on a show, be grand, whatever you like. Be proud of your accomplishments and show it off.**

16.5.2 STUDENT PREPARATION

Everything should be ready and you should be prepared for your speech.

- You have practiced sufficiently out loud.

- You have your speech or notes in hand if needed.

- The video camera is running.

16.5.3   LESSON 12 EXERCISE/SPEECH

Exercise

No exercise is necessary for this lesson.

Speech – Graduation Speech

1. When announced, take a deep breath and step briskly onto stage.

2. Give your audience a welcome smile and launch into your speech.

3. Use all the speaking tools you've learned and **give them your best effort!**

Step forth and be a proud Gabberz!

16.6 ANALYSIS & SCORING

Hand the Analysis and Scoring Sheet to your audience as soon as you have completed your speech event.

Your **Self-Assessment Checklist** follows that. Finally, we show you how you can get a beautiful **Gabberz Level 1 Public Speaking Graduation Certificate** on the page following your self-assessment.

ANALYSIS & SCORING SHEETS – LESSON 12

INSTRUCTIONS FOR AUDIENCE SCORING:

Audience Members: *please work together to score the speaker in the identified categories.*

AUDIENCE: Rank the following categories from 1 to 5: 1 = Needs Work/Strongly Disagree 3 = Average/Agree 5 = Excellent/Strongly Agree	1 to 5
Speech	
The Speaker prepared an event for the audience and made us feel welcome.	
The Speaker appeared prepared and did more than just read a speech.	
The Speaker smiled appropriately during the speech.	
The Speaker was conscientious about making eye contact and connecting with the audience.	
The Speaker talked clearly and at proper volume.	
The Speaker varied tone, pitch, and pace to make the speech interesting and engaging.	
[For audience who has seen multiple speeches] The Speaker has improved significantly since the first speech I saw.	
I enjoyed the speech event and had a good time.	
Comments:	

SELF-ASSESSMENT BY THE STUDENT:

Please rank yourself so that you can see how you improve over time.

STUDENT: Rank the following categories from 1 to 5: 1 = Needs Work/Strongly Disagree 3 = Average/Agree 5 = Excellent/Strongly Agree	1 to 5
The International Space Station did not fall from orbit and crush me on stage.	
I felt prepared and ready when the time came.	
I was comfortable looking the audience members in the eyes and interacting with them.	
I used the 4 P's to interact with my audience and engage them in my speech.	
My notes were easy to follow and helped me keep my place throughout the speech.	
I spent sufficient time practicing and had no problem presenting a 6-minute speech.	
I was not nervous or embarrassed while giving the speech.	
I was excited about giving this speech.	
I had fun and enjoyed giving this speech.	
Comments:	

Do you want a beautiful Gabberz Level 1 Public Speaking Graduation Certificate?

Check out how to get one on the next page!

Public Speaking for Kids, Tweens, and Teens – Confidence for Life!

16.7 CONGRATULATIONS GRADUATE!

Congratulations on completing Level 1 of the program. You are definitely on your way to becoming a **Gabberz Master Speaker**!

Would you like a beautiful, framable Graduation Certificate for Level 1?

All you need to do is upload at least 6 of your lesson videos to YouTube and mention "**Gabberz Public Speaking**" in the description, then let us know.

Here's how:

1. **Upload 6 or more** of your lesson videos to www.YouTube.com and make public.

2. Mention "**Gabberz Public Speaking**" in the description.

3. Email student@gabberz.com and give us **links to the 6 or more videos you publically posted**.

4. Provide your full name and your physical mailing address and we'll send a beautiful certificate at no charge in your name that is suitable for framing. (If you'd prefer an emailed PDF instead, just let us know.)

Public Speaking for Kids, Tweens, and Teens – Confidence for Life!

Gabberz®

www.gabberz.com

Gabberz Public Speaking for Kids, Tweens, and Teens
Level 1, Single-Student, Do-it-Yourself

APPENDIX A

INTRODUCTORY SPEECH

(CHAPTER 4)

INSTRUCTION PAGE—READ ME FIRST

CHAPTER 4, INTRODUCTORY SPEECH (LEVEL 1-0A)

Welcome to your first Gabberz speech!

First we'll give you a little instruction, then **the speech you are to read is on the following pages**. Please follow the instructions carefully to get the most out of the speech.

Speeches may contain some direction to you. These directions are not read, but tell you what you must do while reading the text. We'll help you out with a few visual clues like this:

Speak only the words formatted like this!

Speak the words when you see text formatted like this.

Don't speak words formatted like these!

[Follow Direction, but don't say the words when you see text like this in brackets.]

CHARACTER CHANGE WHEN YOU SEE TEXT LIKE THIS FOR A MULTIPLE CHARACTER SPEECH. DO NOT SAY THE NAME UNLESS DIRECTED TO DO SO.

Footnotes[1] (see below) are not spoken.

Don't worry, you'll get the hang of it quickly. We'll make it as simple as possible. Besides, generally there's not a wrong way to do the prepared speeches. **Just relax, have fun, and improvise if you like.**

One last thing; when you get up, feel free to say something like, **"Good Evening, my speech tonight is titled "_____"**. Or not. Your choice.

Now, let's get started. Your speech starts on the next page.

---

[1] Don't speak the footnotes, they're only there if you want to do some research.

LEVEL 1-0A, INTRODUCTORY SPEECH

"ONE NATION DEDICATED TO CHEESE"

[Speak slow, pause for dramatic effect. Speech should be 2 to 3 minutes. If it comes out shorter, speak slower and/or do things for dramatic effect such as movements and gestures. Try something like walking from one side of the stage to the other between each paragraph. Or maybe pause with your hand to your chin to think. Mix it up. Use your imagination.]

[Use a strong, <u>Presidential</u> voice. If you've heard actors do Abraham Lincoln's voice, try to imitate that. If not, think back on some other speakers with strong, very dramatic speech deliveries. If that doesn't work for you, just use your imagination and try to deliver the speech in as powerful or dramatic a voice as you can.]

[Remember, for this lesson, reading is okay. Speeches are modified.]

[Begin!]

2 Fourscore and seven years ago, our Fathers brought forth on this continent a **new nation**, conceived in Liberty and dedicated to building a cheese factory on the moon.

[Some words and cheeses are highlighted in bold capital letters. Whenever you come to one of these, put a stronger accent on it.]

3 But why, some say, the moon? Why **BLUE CHEESE** as our goal? We choose to make **ROMANO** on the moon in this decade and do the other things, not because **EDAM** is easy, but because **EDAM** is **GOUDA**.

---

2 Abraham Lincoln, "The Gettysburg Address", 1863.
3 John F. Kennedy, Speech at Rice University, 1962.

4 This is preeminently the time for the lactose intolerant to speak the truth, the whole truth, frankly and boldly. So let me assert my firm *BRIE-lief that the only thing we have to FETA is CHEDDAR itself.

5 Therefore, let me say that... I have a CREAM CHEESE, that we will one day live in a nation where LIMBURGER will **not** be judged by its odor, but by the **content** of its flavor.

6 Yesterday—a date which will be served with GOAT CHEESE—we were suddenly and deliberately attacked by NACHO and *QUESO from the MUENSTER of JARLSBERG.

So, we choose to go to the moon. Our NACHO-ral response to this cheesy attack. Once on the moon, we must say...

7 That's one small FETA for man; but one giant HAVARTI for mankind.

---

4 Franklin D. Roosevelt, First Inaugural Address, 1933.
5 Martin Luther King, Jr., Speech on the Lincoln Memorial, 1963.
6 Franklin D. Roosevelt, "Day of Infamy" speech, 1941.
7 Neil Armstrong, NASA Recording Apollo 11, 1969.

*BRIE
[pronounced "bree"]

*QUESO
[pronounced "kay-so"]

8 And so, my fellow Americans, ask **not** what your *BEAUFORT can do for you—ask what **you** can do for your **ROQUEFORT**!   Because...

9 You can eat all the **PARMESAN** some of the time and some of the **PROVOLONE** all of the time, but you **cannot** eat all the **MOZZARELLA** all the time.

10 But has the last **STILTON** been said? Must *BEAUFORT disappear? Is **CAMEMBERT** final? **No!**

[This would be a good time to step forward and use a raised fist for emphasis (maybe each time you say "shall".]

11 We **shall** go on to the end, we **shall** fight in France, we **shall** fight on the **BLUE CHEESE** and *ASIAGOs, we **shall** fight with growing mold, we **shall** fight in the hills; **we shall never GORGONZOLA ! ! !**

And ultimately, men will rise up with power exclaiming "**Give me liber-BRIE** or give me death!"

---

8 John F. Kennedy, Inaugural Speech, 1961.
9 Abraham Lincoln, 1858, and others (still in debate as to the original source of the quote).
10 Charles de Gaulle, "The Appeal of 18 June", 1940.
11 Winston Churchill, Speech to House of Commons, 1940.

*BEAUFORT
[pronounced "bow-fort"]

*ASIAGO
[pronounced "ah-see-ah-go(s)"]

www.gabberz.com

Gabberz Public Speaking for Kids, Tweens, and Teens
Level 1, Single-Student, Do-it-Yourself

APPENDIX B

LESSON 1 SPEECH
(CHAPTER 5)

Public Speaking for Kids, Tweens, and Teens – Confidence for Life!

Gabberz®

INSTRUCTION PAGE—READ ME FIRST

LESSON 1, SEALED SPEECH (LEVEL 1-1A)

Please read these instructions <u>prior</u> to speech day.

This is a sealed speech, so don't peek before you are standing in front of your audience.

The speech must be given with **very exaggerated emotions**. You will be told what emotions to use while reading within the text of the speech. You can pause to read, but be quick.

*Emotional instructions should **not** be read out loud and will look like this:*

_____

[Follow Emotional Directions, but <u>don't</u> say the words out loud when you see text like this in brackets.] _____

Don't speak words formatted like these!

You must speak the words that are in normal text like this:

_____

Speak the words when you see text formatted like this.

_____

Speak only the words formatted like this!

As you open the speech package, be very theatrical about it, saying something like, "***I've never seen what's in here before, so I'm not sure what's going to happen.***"

First, there is a short note you must read to your audience, then you can turn the page and begin.

STOP HERE!

Don't read the speech until it's time for your event.

Have Fun!

Public Speaking for Kids, Tweens, and Teens – Confidence for Life!

LESSON 1 SPEECH

"FAMILY VACATION TIME"

SEALED SPEECH
DO NOT READ
BEFORE SPEECH
TIME!

[read normally]

> We used to be normal people who took normal vacations. You know, air conditioning, swimming pools, that kind of thing.

[shake head <u>sadly</u> and <u>sigh</u>]

> Then Dad got weird. He decided we we're going on an epic, remember-forever vacation.

> Dad over-loaded the minivan with everything we had and refused to tell us where we were going.

[get real over-<u>excited</u>, <u>dance</u>]

> *I'm* thinking Disney, the beach, water parks. This is supposed to be an **epic** vacation after all.

> So we start driving...

[start to get <u>worried</u>]

> and driving... and driving... and driving...

> Till finally we arrive...

[big dramatic <u>pause</u> and <u>yell</u> in dismay]

Camping ? ? ?

[really annoying <u>whine</u>]

> Nooooooo! NOT camping!
>
> Not out in the woods with bears and snakes and poison whatevers...

[get <u>down on knees</u> and <u>beg</u>]

> We can't go camping! We'll never survive.
>
> Everyone knows Bigfoot is out here.
>
> They love to eat tasty, tender little kids like me.

[<u>stand up</u> and shrug grandly]

> As we all know, begging never works.   [big <u>smile</u>]
>
> So... camping it is.
>
> I put on my happy face, but inside I was crying.

[start <u>crying</u> dramatically, act it out]

> No swimming pool. No air conditioning.
>
> Not a restaurant or pizza in sight anywhere.
>
> No beds with sheets and covers.
>
> Just sleeping bags on the ground with bugs and things.

[<u>cry</u> even louder]

> Did they forget about Bigfoot?
>
> Don't they know <u>how good</u> I would taste?

[dramatically pull yourself together]

Okay... I probably won't get eaten by Bigfoot.

[act very <u>startled</u> and look <u>left</u>]

What's that?

[act very <u>scared</u>]

A bear? A mountain lion? A real lion?

Killer monkeys with sharp, pointy teeth?

What can I do to **not** be tasty?

[<u>relax</u> and smile]

Oh, it's just a deer. Cute!

I bet he's more tasty than I am...

Dad interrupted my thoughts with a suggestion.

[<u>whine</u> suddenly]

Hiking?

But there's nature out there.

[act very <u>tired</u>]

Of course, whining didn't work.

We must have hiked a hundred miles.

[<u>smile</u> a little]

But we did see a lot of cool stuff.

[start to get <u>excited</u>]

Oh, and when we got back we roasted hotdogs.

On a stick over this huge fire we built.

[very excited, <u>wave arms, act this out</u>]

And we told scary stories around the fire.

Dad told one about campers lost in the woods.

We all moved closer to the fire.

Then Mom made S'mores.

We ate a bunch!

[act <u>tired</u> and <u>stretch arms</u>]

Finally, it was time to sleep, but I didn't want to.

Although, sleeping in the tent might be kinda' fun.

[<u>smile</u> and <u>shrug</u>]

Okay, so maybe a family camping trip is not so
bad after all. Maybe it is a trip to remember.

[big <u>smile</u>]

Besides, I know we're safe.

I left some S'mores by the fire for Bigfoot.

[take a big <u>bow</u>]

The end!

www.gabberz.com

Gabberz Public Speaking for Kids, Tweens, and Teens
Level 1, Single-Student, Do-it-Yourself

APPENDIX C

LESSON 5 SPEECH
(CHAPTER 9)

INSTRUCTION PAGE—READ ME FIRST

LESSON 5 SPEECH (LEVEL 1-5A)

Please read these instructions _prior_ to speech day.

You will give this speech **twice** <u>as instructed in the lesson</u>.

The first time will be an exercise where you will read it WITHOUT the stage directions in brackets.

The second time must be given with <u>**exaggerated emotions**</u>. You will also need to do as instructed in the **Vocal Directions** in brackets [i.e., screech like a monkey].

Vocal Directions should **not** be read out loud and will look like this:

[Follow Vocal Directions, but <u>don't</u> say the words out loud when you see text like this in brackets.]

You must speak the words that are in normal text like this:

Speak the words when you see text formatted like this.

Be sure to do the lesson as instructed in Chapter 9. Practicing out loud will be important for you to really give this one some character. Remember, you are telling a "story" of adventure.

Have Fun!

LESSON 5 SPEECH

"PRICELESS"

[Remember, <u>don't read the stuff in brackets out loud</u>, those are only directions for you.]

[act confused, questioning]

Silver? Spices? Silly string? Jack the merchant sat at his usual table wondering what to sell next when a hand fell on his shoulder.

[yell "BAM" and smack this paper loudly]

A fellow trader named Andrew sat down. **[yell, "Waiter!"]** Shrimp please. And lobster. And your finest triple-chocolate sundae for my friend."

"Uhh..." said Jack. Money was too tight these days for luxuries like triple-chocolate sundaes.

Andrew smiled. "Don't worry. It's on me."

[laugh like an evil genius]

"In that case, make it two."

Andrew leaned back. "Have I got a *tale* for you. Picture this...

[add strong emotions and movement, he's describing a terrible storm]

Thundering clouds crashing overhead. Pounding waves. A screaming crew **[screech like a monkey]**, a

crying captain, ship rocking back and forth, and me turning green, looking for a bucket so I could—"

Jack held up a hand. "Can we skip ahead?"

"Right." Andrew cleared his throat. "When the clouds parted and the heaving stopped, we glimpsed an uncharted island. It looked like a good **[snort really loud like a hog]** place to run aground."

"The islanders took us to a palace brimming with palm trees, parrots, and pistachios." Andrew sighed. "How I love pistachios..."

Jack tapped his fingers impatiently.

"Anyway," continued Andrew **[shout "Arrrrr" like a pirate]**, "when the king heard I was a merchant, he was eager to trade. 'We could use some timber,' he said. Then the King jumped when a mouse squeaked behind his throne.

'I'm sorry. We don't have any timber,' I replied.

'Cloth? Dyes? Hula hoops?' asked the **[make a sound like an ambulance siren]** king.

'We have fish,' I offered, as a mouse skittered over my boot.

The king raised his eyebrow. 'As do we.'

An island. Right. I tried again. 'We have furs.'

As he shook a mouse off his pant legs, the king raised his other eyebrow in annoyance. A tropical island. Right. Then it came to me. 'We have [bray like a donkey] cats.'

'What are cats?' asked the king.

'They are cute and furry,' I explained, '**AND they catch mice**.'

'What would you like in exchange for these marvelous creatures?' asked the king.

[blow hard like a hurricane wind]

How could I charge for a bunch of stray cats? 'Your hospitality is enough,' I told him.

But when the king saw how the cats rid the palace of mice, he marched to his treasury and loaded us up with barrels of gold and jewels. And pistachios. I do love..."

"I know," said Jack excitedly. "Where was that island, exactly?"

Jack loaded his ship with timber, cloth, dye, and hula hoops. [yell "yee-haw" like a cowboy] If the king had rewarded Andrew for some cats he didn't even know he wanted, just imagine what he'd give Jack for the stuff he *did* want.

Jack and his crew set sail. Soon, [moo loudly like a cow] they arrived at the island. The king was pleased to have another trader – and carrying exactly the things he wanted.

"What can we offer in exchange?" asked the king.

"Nothing, your majesty," said Jack as humbly as possible. "I am happy to be of service."

The king shook his head. "You must be repaid for your generous treasures."

Jack could barely contain himself. He had plenty of room on the ship for barrels full of gold and jewels.

The king said, "I have something of **tremendous** value I'd like to share with you. Something **priceless**, in fact."

[yell "Jackpot!"]

Jack could not believe his luck.

And then, the king handed him a basket full of cats.

[take a big bow]

The end!

www.gabberz.com

Gabberz Public Speaking for Kids, Tweens, and Teens
Level 1, Single-Student, Do-it-Yourself

APPENDIX D

LESSON 9 SPEECH
(CHAPTER 13)

INSTRUCTION PAGE—READ ME FIRST

LESSON 9, PACING SPEECH (LEVEL 1-9A)

Welcome to your next Gabberz speech!

Patrick Henry's speech is one of the most famous of all time, and one of the most passionate. We're going to help you bring some of that passion to your presentation of this speech.

As with previous speeches, we've provided some instruction to you within the speech. You can follow those directions [the smaller bold words in **brackets**], but should not read them out loud.

Feel free to modify any of the instructions as the muse drives you. It's your speech, so do what feels right to you to help you build a connection with your audience.

We'll help you out with a few visual clues like this:

Speak the words when you see text formatted like this.

Speak only the words formatted like this!

[Follow Direction, but don't say the words when you see text like this in brackets.]

Don't speak words formatted like these!

It's important that you **practice a lot** to really bring the speech to life and inspire your audience with your passion and pacing.

Don't worry, you'll get the hang of it quickly. We'll make it as simple as possible. Besides, generally there's not a wrong way to do the prepared speeches. **Just relax, have fun, and improvise all you like.**

Now, let's get started. Your speech starts on the next page.

LESSON 9A, PACING SPEECH

"GIVE ME PACING, OR GIVE MY SPEECH DEATH"

(650 Words <u>loosely</u> based on Patrick Henry's speech to the VA Convention on March 23, 1775.)

[Look around the audience and begin speaking quietly, but with power.]

No man thinks more highly than I do of the patriotism, as well as abilities, of the **<u>very worthy gentlemen</u>** who have just addressed the House.

[Pause, shake head, possibly point at a few individuals.]

But different men often see the things in different lights; and, therefore, [pause] I shall speak forth my sentiments freely and [raise voice] without reserve.

[pause, take deep breath] It is only in [emphasis] **<u>this</u>** way that we can hope to arrive at truth, and fulfill the great responsibility which we hold to our country.

[slowly speed pace through paragraph to build emotion.]

Should I keep back my opinions at such a time, [pause] through fear of giving offense, I should consider myself as [strong emphasis] **<u>guilty of treason</u>** towards my country.

[Take a deep breath, let it out in a sigh, then continue.]

Mr. President, [pause] [pause] it is natural to men to indulge in the [look negative and shake head] illusions of hope. We are apt to shut our eyes against a **<u>painful</u>** truth, and listen to the song of that siren [say with disdain/anger] till she *transforms us into beasts.*